# Light of the World

# Light of the World
# Daily Readings for Advent

Peter Millar and Neil Paynter

WILD GOOSE PUBLICATIONS

First published 2009 by
Wild Goose Publications,
4th Floor, Savoy House, 140 Sauchiehall St, Glasgow G2 3DH, UK.
Wild Goose Publications is the publishing division of the Iona Community.
Scottish Charity No. SCO03794. Limited Company Reg. No. SCO96243.
www.ionabooks.com

ISBN 978-1-905010-63-9

Cover photo © David Coleman

The publishers gratefully acknowledge the support of the Drummond Trust,
3 Pitt Terrace, Stirling FK8 2EY in producing this book.

Overseas distribution:
Australia: Willow Connection Pty Ltd, Unit 4A, 3-9 Kenneth Road,
Manly Vale, NSW 2093
New Zealand: Pleroma, Higginson Street, Otane 4170, Central Hawkes Bay
Canada: Novalis/Bayard Publishing & Distribution, 10 Lower Spadina Ave.,
Suite 400, Toronto, Ontario M5V 2Z2

Printed by Bell & Bain, Thornliebank, Glasgow

**Mixed Sources**
Product group from well-managed
forests and other controlled sources
www.fsc.org   Cert no. TT-COC-002769
© 1996 Forest Stewardship Council
FSC

# CONTENTS

6

8

# INTRODUCTION

Advent is a time for reflection, of lighting the candles. A time of preparation, of waiting, of expectancy. A time for thinking about our personal journey as a human being held in God's love, and also a time for thinking about God's world. It is a time when God's Spirit, working through our lives each day, challenges our easy assumptions about life and belief, and allows us space to turn away from these surface things which constantly delude our inner life. Traditionally in the days of Advent there has been an emphasis on the coming of Light – that Light which illumines all our journeys and brings healing to the nations.

I have always been inspired by the words, 'God matters: God's world matters: We matter to God.' Although these words are not specifically for Advent, they express succinctly a central meaning of the weeks leading up to Christmas in the liturgical year. In this book, the writers take seriously, and also joyfully, the fact that this is God's world, and that our theologies and spiritualities, rooted in Christ, are earthed in daily realities. In the confusions, passions, energies and longings of every day.

The Iona Community, begun in Scotland but now touching the lives of many around the world, has always believed that our Christian faith and what is happening in society are interconnected. Or to put it another way: everyday living and worship go hand in hand. So in these pages, the biblical texts, which relate to Advent, give birth to a range of issues. These include peace and justice, the joys and sorrows of daily life, the spiritual life, the cries of our wounded earth, risk-taking, relationships, questions of faith, political and social issues, the Holy Spirit, the search for hope in a violent world, and much more.

Each reflection provides a starting point for our own thoughts. The book can be read in many ways. Dipped into, read through, or used with a single reflection for each day. What matters is that God who holds the world in his or her hands becomes alive, each day, in our hearts. That the Christ who was born in Palestine all these centuries ago, will, in the present time, open our minds to new possibilities, alternative directions and to fresh ways of perceiving our world.

Advent is a special time in the Christian year. In our troubled world, which is also a world of extraordinary possibility and creativity, we perhaps need such times more than ever. Times to renew our soul so that our lives may express a deeper compassion and a more joy-filled awareness. Or in the beautiful words of the old Eastern Orthodox prayer: *Set our hearts on fire with love to thee, O Christ, that in that flame we may love thee and our neighbour as ourselves.*

May these pages enlarge our hope, and bring us to Christmas morning with Christ's light steadily illumining our path.

Peter Millar

# NOVEMBER 27

In the messiness and beauty of the here and now

*Rejoice, daughter of Zion! I am coming; I shall make my dwelling among you, says the Lord.*

Zechariah 2:10

If you asked people on the street, 'Do you know what the word incarnate means?' few would know. 'Incarnate' and 'Incarnation' are not words we often hear. At least not on the streets around me! Yet, if we look at recent statistics there are still many people (perhaps surprisingly) in these same streets who believe that there is a God, and that He or She is with us in our lives – aware of our needs and longings. A God who is somehow present on earth.

In the traditional Christian creeds we talk of God becoming 'incarnate' – meaning 'made one with us'. In the weeks of Advent we prepare our thoughts in a particular way for this God's coming into our midst in the person of Jesus Christ. I have always valued that spiritual understanding of 'the expectant heart' – the heart waiting and willing to be surprised again by the wind of the Spirit; for our lives to be taken into a new place of spiritual awareness as we look towards that birth in Bethlehem 2000 years ago. The prophecy of Zechariah, made centuries earlier, is to be made real. As the old hymn says:

*Hark the glad sound! The Saviour comes,*
*the Saviour promised long;*
*let every heart exult with joy,*
*and every heart with song!*

In recent years there has been a lot of discussion about atheism. That debate had engaged the minds of many people, and I have followed it with interest for I know how hard it is for many to believe in God. When I was living on the island of Iona, I often thought back to Saint Columba and his small group of monks who had arrived on the island in 563 AD. What struck me was their deep belief in 'the presence' of God. Every aspect of their daily living was shot through with the knowledge (not just head knowledge) that they were embraced in a wider Love: that nothing could separate them from that Love: that ultimately all creation would be held in that Love. And their way of life, rooted in their prayers, expressed this belief with powerful clarity.

If God was only an abstract concept then I too would be among those who say that they find belief difficult. But these ordinary, yet extraordinary, people who came to Iona all these years ago – and not only them – have brought home to me the reality of a God who dwells in our midst. In life – in the messiness and beauty of the here and now. Of course much of this I don't understand – it's a mystery, but I do believe enough to know that I am held in a wider Love, and that God infuses meaning into my existence here on earth.

Through all of life's questions, we remain enfolded in a mantle of Love.

A good friend, the late Chandran Devanesan of South India, expressed this awareness with great tenderness:

*O Thou, who has given me eyes to see the light that fills my room, give me the inward vision to behold Thee in this place.*

Peter Millar

# NOVEMBER 28

All things are possible

*See, the former things have come to pass, and new things I now declare …*

Isaiah 42:9

*Jesus looked at them and said: 'For mortals it is impossible, but for God all things are possible.'*

Matthew 19:26

*He said: 'Abba, Father, for you all things are possible …'*

Mark 14:36

For the generations who have grown up with the internet, the iPhone, space travel and the mapping of the human genome, it's not really surprising to be tempted to imagine that, for us mortals, all things are possible. Surely one day, in the not too distant future, we'll be able to end wars, cure cancer, control climate change, and feed the world?

That these things are actually possible; that we mortals now have – or can get – the knowledge and skill to bring them to pass; this is not in doubt. But what is in doubt – some would put it stronger – is the mortal will to work together to make them happen.

The good news of Advent is about the coming into human life of the God who makes all things new – and all things possible – by striking at the heart of humanity. God does this, not like some magician producing wonderful tricks out of a hat, or like some advertising corporation promising the impossible, but by inviting us first to reflect on 'the former things that have come to pass' – by asking us, in other words, to view, with the eyes of faith, God's own track record, and then act accordingly.

For what has God already done? Created the universe out of nothing. Breathed life into mortals, and planted within us the knowledge of God, and of the good, more deeply than all that is wrong. Given us to know that we are made to live not alone but in community, and shown us what God requires of us – to do justice, to love kindness and to walk humbly with God.

All this, God has already done. And now, waiting in Advent, we sense that God does the one thing more that is needed. God comes in Jesus, the Compassion, the Forgiveness, and the present and living Power of God. So God enables us to will, and to do, what is indeed impossible for mortals – to open our hearts and our arms to each other, to tear down the walls of force and of fear that separate us, and to work with God to 'make all things new'.

Prayer

*Living God,*
*your ways are indeed not our ways,*
*nor your thoughts our thoughts.*

*We look back,*
*with pride in what we have achieved;*
*you ask us to look back*
*in wonder at what you have done.*

*We look forward,*
*conscious of our need,*
*and cautiously confident in ourselves;*
*you ask us to look forward,*
*to know your will for all creation,*
*and to put our trust in you.*

*But most of all, this Advent, we pray:*
*give us the grace to live in the present moment;*
*to welcome your coming in Jesus,*
*and to attend to what we must now do.*
*So may our impossibilities*
*become your possibilities,*
*in the new things that you will bring to birth*
*in our world.*

*We pray in Jesus' name.*
*Amen*

John Harvey

# NOVEMBER 29

Signs of peace and life-giving joy

*How wonderful it is, how pleasant for God's people to live together in harmony.*

Psalm 133:1

Sometimes it's hard to see signs of peace and life-giving joy in our violent world. But they are there. And in often surprising places. Small signs that reach far beyond their local context. The kind of signs that make us halt in our tracks and make us ponder. Signs that take us on a different road. Signs that refresh us.

Take the 'Four Sikhs in the City'*, for example. They are marathon runners. Nothing unusual in that you say! Well, perhaps there is. For Amrik Singh is 79, Kamil Singh is 80, Ajit Singh is 79 – and Fauja Singh is 98. Together, these Sikh friends have become something of a celebrity group as they take part in marathons, not only in the UK but also overseas.

Fauja exudes a boyish charm and a level of fitness that makes you forget he's close to 100. He first ran as a young man in India, and returned to the sport after a 54-year gap – at the age of 89! He took up running after losing a son and, later, his wife – losses which left him demoralised and saddened and in need of a new focus in life. He soon began to challenge other OAPs to races. In an interview he chuckled cheekily when he explained how he increased his competitive edge: 'If they looked healthy, I'd extend the distance; the races got longer and longer, until I ran my first official race – a 20 km run for cancer research – in 1999.'

As these four great guys run in various races, they do more than just cover the distance. They carry hope and energy and inspiration. Everywhere they go they find huge acknowledgement and a warm welcome. Young and old alike admire their commitment, but also warm to their smiling faces and exuberance. Just reading about them lifted my heart.

Amrik, Fauja, Ajit and Kamil are in their own astonishing way peace-bearers and encouragers for many others. They brighten our world and open our eyes to new possibilities. Their running has raised lots of money for good causes and countless small signs of peace in our turbulent world. And I am sure they have many miles still to go!

Prayer

*Lord, in these weeks of waiting for You*
*help us to be touched*
*by all the small signs of peace and joy*
*which are*
*in our midst.*

Peter Millar

*\* The title of an article*

# NOVEMBER 30

The Word

*And the Word became flesh and lived among us …*

John 1:14

People come to Iona from all over the world to volunteer. Most often from Western countries – America, Canada, Australia, Germany, Sweden… but sometimes from so-called 'developing' nations.

One year when I was working on the Resident group, two women came from Sudan. Felicia and Mercy (not their real names) were friends of an Iona Community member who had worked in Sudan and Uganda for many years.

Not long after they arrived, Mercy and Felicia said that they would like to make an African meal for all the volunteers and residents. They wanted to do something to thank everyone for being so warm and welcoming. So they got together with Anja and Helen, the Abbey cooks, and made a big pot of of a seedy and meaty stew, which they served with a kind of flat bread called *kissra*. It was a great evening. We got a cassette of African music from the community shop and danced in the refectory. Later we drummed and sang in the Relig Oran – African songs and Wild Goose chants – the sound of jembes echoing in the 12th-century chapel, and swirling and drifting out into the ancient graveyard.

One day, not long after guests started arriving at the centres, the women said that they would like to lead a justice and peace service about the situation in their country, and asked me to help them put it together – they wanted people in the West to know what was happening in Sudan. They hadn't seen anything in the newspaper or on television about it: Thousands of people were dying or being made homeless – and all they had seen was a programme called *Who Wants To Be a Millionaire* and something called *Big Brother*.

Felicia, Mercy and I got together one night, and ended up putting together a service of letters: Felicia and Mercy had received an email from the minister of their church in Sudan – a few days after helicopter gunships had strafed their village; there was an email from the women back to their minister; and I'd found letters from aid agencies on the internet, calling for the immediate delivery of food aid and medicine. It became a service about the Word. About hearing God's Word and the cries of our sisters and brothers.

The heart of the service was a testimony by Felicia, who spoke about life at her village church, and the women in the congregation who were trying to set up a co-op. They wanted to sell pottery in the markets, and to fair-trading organisations like Traidcraft.

During the action, the congregation were invited to come to the front of the Abbey church and to write a message to the village church in Sudan: we'd draped a long sheet of brown paper across the communion table. People wrote messages like 'Greetings from Iona, we are thinking of you', 'You are not forgotten', 'Peace be with you', 'We send our love and are with you in spirit' … and children came up and drew pictures of rainbows and puffins and smiling suns, with crayons and magic markers. After writing their messages, folk were invited to take some campaign information away with them (regarding the role of Western oil companies in civil wars in Africa), and to later send letters, emails or faxes to their Member of Parliament.

It was a powerful, moving, inspiring service, and during tea and coffee in the refectory afterwards, someone announced that what was needed now was action – words weren't enough. So a collection was taken for the women's co-op, and later a bank account was set up for donations. When Felicia and Mercy left Iona, they went on a short speaking tour of the UK, staying at Abbey and MacLeod Centre guests' homes across the UK, and talking to their churches.

Prayer

*God, we confess that we often close our ears to your Word,*
*to the messages of your prophets,*
*and to the cries of the poor.*

*We confess that we often pay far more attention*
*to the life-in-all-its-fullness promise of advertisers*
*and the announcements of the rich and famous,*
*to the pronouncements of pop idols and*
*the predictions of sports stars.*
*We confess that we seek to be entertained and comforted*
*and not disturbed and challenged;*
*that we would rather retreat into fantasy worlds*
*than engage with reality, and the tortured earth's suffering people;*
*that we prefer sound bites and sensationalism*
*to long, difficult stories of everyday pain and struggle,*
*faith and courage, great sacrifice and*
*precious, hard-won gains.*

*God, we confess that, close to home, we are often gossipy*
*and talk about our neighbours without any real understanding or compassion.*

*We confess that we take our freedom of expression for granted,*
*and loudly voice a great many strong views and opinions*
*concerning matters which seem important,*
*while, at other times, we are afraid to speak out about the slightest thing*
*that might single us out or bring trouble.*

*Meantime, our sisters and brothers across the world are silenced with bullets,*
*or are shut up in dark prisons for voicing opposition and calling for change –*
*for demanding that basic human rights be respected.*

*God, open our ears to the cries of your people,*
*to the warnings of your prophets,*
*and to your good news.*

*Open our hearts to our neighbours*
*and help us to love them as Jesus taught us.*

*God, help us to hear your voice through the babble of this world*
*where words are used to confuse, distract, manipulate, sell illusion, buy power;*
*help us to be still and receptive to your healing,*
*encouraging,*
*inspiring,*
*enduring,*
*life-giving*
*Word …*

Blessing from the Abbey service for Sudan

*May God write a message upon your heart,*
*bless and direct you,*
*then send you out –*
*living letters of the Word.*
*Amen*

Neil Paynter

# DECEMBER 1

A counter-cultural vision for our times

*The Shoot of Jesse will judge the poor with justice, the meek with equity, and the wolf will lie down with the lamb.*

Isaiah 11:5–6

What a counter-cultural vision in our times! As we come to Advent and to this vision of Isaiah, we can look back over the past year in our interconnected world, and be reminded of the trillions of pounds and dollars which have floated away, through human greed, in the financial crisis. Of bankers and others earning sums of money beyond the dreams of avarice: of our leaders desperately trying to create visions of justice while themselves constantly at the service of the powerful. No wonder millions everywhere are disillusioned. Are we surprised that cynicism abounds?

In this passage (Isaiah 11:1–11) we are reminded of the coming of a scion of the line of David (The Shoot of Jesse) who would exhibit all the qualities a king was ideally supposed to have. Propelled by God's spirit, this leader would hold in himself wisdom, right resolution (and the ability to act upon it) and practical piety. Such a leader would not be relying on outward appearances, but would espouse the cause of the weak and confront those who oppressed them. And it was in this tenacious hope, often not realised, that the Messianic expectations of Israel had its roots.

And as we read our daily papers many of us must say: 'Does not our world desperately need such leaders who speak from the heart, who listen to the oppressed and who are humble enough to admit to their own failings?' And we need such women and men not just in politics but across the board – offering a new vision of what it means to be human in a world which, despite all the technological advances, often feels a very uncertain and scary place.

Yet the text also addresses us as individuals. These powerful words frame a communal vision while at the same time calling us to carry within our own lives that combination of integrity, resolution and hope. Inviting us always to be listeners of the world. The question which always returns to us concerns our hearts and minds being alive to what is going on around us in God's world. And for those who claim to be trying to follow the way of the Gospel, withdrawal is not an option.

The Australian theologian Dorothy McRae-McMahon, who constantly inspires my own spiritual journey, once wrote:

*We believe in the Holy Spirit who waits on our moments of openness and springs into the unknowns with joy and delight, that we might be called on beyond where we thought we could go, where every step is walked on holy ground.*

Powerful words, and ones which for me mirror something of that age-old vision of the prophet Isaiah.

Peter Millar

# DECEMBER 2

A pair of secateurs

*For he grew up before him like a young plant,*
*and like a root out of dry ground;*
*he had no form or majesty that we should look at him,*
*nothing in his appearance that we should desire him.*

Isaiah 53:2

'I am the true vine, and my Father is the vinegrower. He removes every branch in me that bears no fruit. Every branch that bears fruit he prunes to make it bear more fruit. You have already been cleansed by the word that I have spoken to you. Abide in me as I abide in you. Just as the branch cannot bear fruit by itself unless it abides in the vine, neither can you unless you abide in me. I am the vine, you are the branches.*

John 15:1–4

The Pilsdon Community in Dorset, inspired by the 17th-century community of Little Gidding, welcomes people to a working household based on worship and shared meals. Many guests have been bruised and broken by 21st-century society, and find Pilsdon a safe place where healing can happen. I went there for a time of reflection at the beginning of Advent, and to learn more about its hands-on ministry. After a mug of tea, the first thing I was given was a pair of secateurs: the espalier trees in the old walled garden needed pruning. So, for a whole winter afternoon, that is what I did. It's a good way to reflect on what needs attention in your own life!

Espalier

*Stretched across the wall,*
*tied on wires,*
*pruned back hard,*
*as the year*
*shrinks to the shortest day:*
*this apple tree*
*seems barely alive –*
*a thing of no beauty, a travesty.*

*But believe me*
*there is more to this story,*
*these bare bones:*
*one spring day*
*these knuckles will flex,*
*and send out shoots,*
*form buds, open green leaves*
*against the red brick wall;*
*flowers will beckon the bees,*
*and fruit ripen*
*on a tree stretched to its limits now –*
*but still fully alive.*

*Pilsdon Manor, 1.12.08*

Jan Sutch Pickard

# DECEMBER 3

Creatively surviving

*For the Lord is a God of justice; blessed are all those who wait for him.*

Isaiah 30:18

When I was employed as a mental health support worker, I used to visit a young man who lived in a tower block in a rough area of Edinburgh. I'd visit and see how his week went, find out if he had enough groceries, what bills needed to be paid … and we'd just sit and drink tea and talk. His flat had been broken into three times. He'd been jumped down at the shops and beaten up by a gang who said he was a gay … Every day was hard for him.

He'd had a job long ago, 'in another life', in a museum, but had a nervous breakdown, and with no support – no family or friends – ended up homeless; then 'trapped in the social work system'.

He did a lot (on top of the list of all the plain, everyday things) just to survive. One thing he'd do was go to charity shops like Oxfam and Save the Children, and buy cheap reproductions of paintings with a portion of his giro money. His flat was full of masterpieces – Monets, Van Goghs, Michelangelos, Seurats, Chagalls, Vermeers, Rembrandts … Underneath, the walls were peeling and water-marked; punched and kicked in by previous tenants. The walls out in the corridor were all graffitied, and echoed when you walked in them: like the building was vacant of soul; there were needles and syringes and empty bottles lying in corners. He'd burn incense in winter to cover up the mouldy-damp smell in his flat. The smell of incense helped 'put him in a better place', he said.

Another thing he'd do to survive was go to the Hermitage, a woods nearby. He explained that some days he felt 'too surrounded by concrete and grey-ness'. He'd go sit under the trees for a few hours. Walk the quiet paths. Look at the wild flowers.

When I asked him why he collected paintings, and took walks in the Her-mitage, he thought a moment, and said: '… It's the way I keep hope alive.'

He was always waiting: waiting to get money from social work to get his broken glasses fixed; waiting for Council Tax to forgive him; waiting to get to the top of the housing list; waiting to win the lottery. Waiting …

One day, in passing, he mentioned that he used to go to church once, years ago. He didn't now. 'Church is for rich people,' he said. His church was his paintings, and walking in the woods at the Hermitage.

He was an artist in creative survival. That's what I loved and appreciated about him – the way he could creatively survive.

Prayer

*God of the cathedral of trees;*
*Creative Christ of the tower block;*
*help us to give support and to bring some understanding and gentleness*
*to people living in areas where life is hard:*

*People waiting to be delivered,*
*from poor housing, intimidation, violence, Council tax bills, loan sharks,*
*depression …*
*Amen*

Neil Paynter

# DECEMBER 4

Taming the Gospel

*They will know that they have a prophet among them, whether they listen or whether in their rebelliousness they refuse to listen.*

Ezekiel 2:5

By and large, prophets are uncomfortable people to be around. They confront and disrupt our comfort zones. Unsettle us. Challenge our assumptions. Renew our vision or take it in another direction. Vincent Van Gogh was such a person – a prophet and visionary. Yet Ben Shahn was right when he wrote: 'It may be a point of pride to have a Van Gogh on the living room wall, but the prospect of having Van Gogh himself in the living room would put a good many devoted art lovers to rout.' Most of us prefer quiet companions to unsettling visionaries.

However, the truth is that without prophetic voices all of us are impoverished – whether it's in the arts, or politics, or education, or in a hundred other areas of life. And we certainly need many prophetic voices if our wounded planet is to healed.

Down through the centuries, the birth of Jesus has often been portrayed in a passive way. Baby Jesus in swaddling clothes, smiling tenderly. And for many people Christian faith is rather like that. Comforting, but never challenging. Pleasant, but certainly never disturbing. All that is desired from faith in Christ is 'quiet peace of mind'. What the psychiatrist Karl Menninger called 'illusory peace'.

Ezekiel is not interested in illusory peace. He was living in exile in Babylon during the period before and after the fall of Jerusalem in 586 BC. His message was both for the exiles and to the people of Jerusalem. He was emphasising the need for inner renewal of heart and spirit, and the responsibility of the individual to look clearly at their own sins and failings. Underlying these warnings was a profound message of hope for both people and for the nation as a whole. It was a call to return to holiness.

In Advent we look forward to the coming of Jesus. The question remains do we actually want this prophet when he comes to disturb us in our daily living? To arouse our anger about the injustices in God's world? To propel us to take risks for truth and to be open about our own vulnerabilities? To be aware that God is calling us to holy, disciplined living? To discover in all the fragmentations of our world a new way to be human?

The late Jock Dalrymple, a priest whose life disturbed and comforted many, expressed it succinctly: *'We are just beginning to get away from the idea that holiness consists in prayer and charity and abstention from involvement in the world's affairs. You can only go so far in taming the Gospel. If you persist in removing its disturbing elements, you wake up one day to find that you have lost the Christian vision altogether.'*

Prayer

*Lord, don't let our palm trees hide us from the world.*

*A prayer from Tahiti*

Peter Millar

# DECEMBER 5

*But when the Samaritan saw him he had compassion.*

Luke 10:33

A letter to a dying child from a church minister

Dear Child,

I saw your picture in the Christian Aid advert this morning. I am sorry you are dying because there's no clean water where you live. For a moment I was quite upset. However, to be frank, I have to say the situation is largely your own fault. For a start, you chose the wrong parents. And the wrong address. As you have probably realised, most of the world's resources are controlled by white people in the northern part of the globe. Part of the problem is you are black and you live in a country most rich people have hardly heard of and care nothing about (unless it can make them more money). Added to which, if you don't mind me saying so, you have a very odd-sounding name. If you were white and called Sally or Gordon and lived in a nice village, say in the Borders or Sussex, people would be much more interested. Have you thought of changing your name or coming to die in Edinburgh – or maybe London? Or perhaps you could become slightly more white? Michael Jackson did it. Palestinians are more white, but not OK white, I admit. They are generally regarded as troublemakers because they want freedom, and you can never understand their accents when they are interviewed on the radio. So they come across as very foreign – like Jesus was. Israelis are really very white and their country gets lots of mentions in the Bible – so that is good news. Anyway: back to your situation. There's also the problem of the way you have chosen to die. The human-interest angle works best if you get killed in a way that looks spectacular on the TV. A train crash is good, and a plane crash even better. Of course the best way to go is to be in a sky-scraper hit by a plane. Yes, I know: more than 25,000 other people in the Third World, including 8,000 children like you, died on 9/11. Yes – and on every day since 9/11. Yes, they were just as precious to God as the people in the Twin Towers. But that just proves my point: you're doing it wrong. I don't suppose there are any skyscrapers where you live?

Look, I realise this is of little help as you die, but maybe you could leave a note for your friends. A few hints on how to get the attention of the Western world and its right-wing media. No, I don't recommend hijacking a plane, though I can see where you're coming from. Meanwhile, I'll put a bit extra in the Christian Aid envelope. Will that help you personally? I suppose not – but it might help your friends. And it will definitely help me sleep better.

Every blessing,

Prayer

*Loving Father, help us to see our neighbour, our sister and our brother in the other person. Help us to see beyond skin colour and nationality; beyond language and religion, tribe and gender. Help us to see with the deep compassion of a heart filled with your love. As we hear the familiar story of the Good Samaritan, help us to be challenged by it. To hear those words of Jesus that we prefer to forget: 'Go and do thou likewise.' Amen*

David Rhodes

# DECEMBER 6

Take light, give light

*Praise the Lord! ...*
*who executes justice for the oppressed;*
*who gives food to the hungry.*

*The Lord sets the prisoner free;*
*the Lord opens the eyes of the blind.*
*The Lord lifts those who are bowed down;*
*the Lord loves the righteous.*
*The Lord watches over the strangers;*
*he upholds the orphan and the widow ...*
*Praise the Lord!*

Psalm 146:1,7–9, 10

'We ourselves feel that what we are doing is just a drop in the ocean. But the
ocean would be less because of that missing drop.'

Mother Teresa

I sat on the aeroplane full of anxiety for the sixteen days ahead. What was I
doing? Whose idea was this? Or more to the point, how did I let myself have
this idea? In front of me I could see the sixteen other members of our team,
mainly young people and young adults from Richmond Team Ministry,
contentedly watching movies and chatting. I, on the other hand, was full of
terror for all of our lives, and for the sense of trust everyone had placed in

us. God help us. I don't think I have ever felt so inadequate for any task. We were heading to Pune, India to engage in voluntary work with the Deep Griha Society. We would spend a week in the urban slum projects and a week in a rural orphanage called City of Child. We had spent the year fundraising for the trip, raising over £15,000 to give directly to the NGO …

## 'I'll die if I don't have a fizzy drink soon'

It was our circle time, our daily meeting to talk about practicalities and about how we were all feeling. This was a comment from one of the young people in the group. I sighed to myself. We were staying in a rural orphanage. We were recipients of real hospitality and generosity. People were going out daily to buy us mineral water so that we would not have to drink the contaminated water the orphans drink. The group was fed up with drinking lukewarm water. They wanted Coke. I simply felt torn in every direction. How can we hold these things together? An awareness of our privilege. A gracious acceptance of hospitality. The dissatisfaction of the group …

## A rich, painful, beautiful glimpse of India

So, which stories do I tell you? Our team in India worked hard and gave their all. We painted a stunning mural in the rooftop classroom in the Bibwewadi slum. We drank chai in people's homes in the slums, met newborn infants, embraced HIV-positive children and saw community work in action. We ran a pioneering community outreach programme in Deep Griha's newest project, the Vidyanagari, or City of Knowledge: Over one hundred children came from the local community to workshops designed and run by our group – the day was a tremendous success, and the first of many to come. We lived and worked alongside the children at City of Child: they taught us Bollywood dances and songs about Jesus; we taught them English, games, sports, crafts and music. We brought T-shirts for them to design. They coloured them beautifully and wore them with pride. We built roads, painted stones, painted gates, dug with pickaxes and planted trees while they were at school. We ran a carousel of activities for them in the evenings after school. We experienced village life, temple worship, a school assembly … We ate with our fingers curries of simple home-grown vegetables. We washed in buckets of cold water. We sat through a cricket tournament in the pouring rain, and I had to present the winning team with the trophy. We were each given a garland of jasmine and marigolds when we finished our volunteer work. We experienced a rich, painful, beautiful glimpse of India …

'Didi!'

One day, while standing on the perimeter wall to paint the top of the mural in the rooftop Deep Griha classroom in the Bibwewadi slum, the children in the alleyway below me were calling to me and waving. 'Didi!' (meaning 'Big sister'), they shouted, laughing. In that one moment, all that mattered was giving my attention to those children. To wave and smile and hear their laughter and giggling and playfulness. There was no result in this exchange. No task to accomplish and no grades given. It was simply about human beings meeting each other. Human beings in impossibly different power relationships; human beings with shockingly unjust differences in wealth and status; human beings who do not speak the same language and who do not even know each other's names. But I was a stranger and I was welcomed. I was called 'Big sister'. I was loved and met in my full humanity. For me, it was a sacrament, and it was Jesus that I met and received in those children. Our call to follow Jesus is about putting down our paintbrushes to wave and smile at Indian children we will never see again, in a moment of divine communion where Christ comes in a group of strangers. It is about holding together the unbearable contrasts of our privilege and wealth and the poverty of our sisters and brothers, who give so much more in every respect. It is about refusing to be overwhelmed and looking the truth in the eye. It is about knowing that what we are doing is only a drop in the ocean, but steadfastly holding on to the foolish belief that every drop matters. One young person who went to India said: 'Although we have only done something very small, I hope the work we did will leave a lasting contribution to lots of people. It has been the most challenging, rewarding and enjoyable trip of my life.' Another said: 'I don't think it was just the children I helped who learned something new. I think that I also learned from the children and adults there as well.'

One of the orphans at City of Child summed this up in the T-shirt he designed. He drew a picture of a lighthouse, the Deep Griha logo. Underneath he wrote four words: *Take Light, Give Light.*

*Deep Griha, meaning 'Lighthouse', is an independent charitable organisation working to better the lives of people in the slums of Pune. Through a range of family welfare programmes, encompassing education, health, awareness- building and self-help projects, DGS helps thousands within Pune and several nearby villages.*

Prayer

*God, you come to us unexpectedly*
*in the hands and voice of a stranger*
*and in the everyday details of our lives.*

*Give us courage to keep working for justice*
*and the grace to give ourselves totally,*
*so that even in small things*
*our lives will make a difference.*
*Amen*

Lotte Webb

# DECEMBER 7

Birthed in places of human violence and oppression

*But we have God's promise, and look forward to new heavens and a new earth, the home of justice.*

2 Peter 3:13

It is in the *New English Bible*, first published in 1961, that we find the words 'the home of justice'. New heavens (in the plural) and a new earth are the places where, ultimately, God's justice will prevail. A reality expressed with such clarity in Archbishop Desmond Tutu's words, written during the years of apartheid in his native South Africa:

*Lord,*
*help us to learn that goodness is stronger than evil:*
*that love is stronger than hate;*
*that light is stronger than darkness;*
*that life is stronger than death.*

Yet as I write this reflection, I know that this ultimate vision of God's justice, which is central to our Advent hope, is far from being realised on this earth. We all know that, even if we never read the daily papers or listen to the news bulletins. My elder son is presently working in Afghanistan, heading up a programme involved with the clearing of landmines in war-torn Helmand Province. Constantly he sees not only his own colleagues wounded, and sometimes killed, by these newly laid landmines, but also the lives of many local people – children, women and men – tragically cut short.

Today, in areas like Helmand Province and in many other situations in our world we cannot speak glibly of new heavens and a new earth. There are too many dimensions of human suffering and sorrow permeating everyday life in such places. Yet I believe there can be, even in the darkest of nights, 'a vision of God's justice' within our minds and souls. Hate is not the last word. 'Light is stronger than darkness.' And such words themselves often are birthed in places of human violence and oppression.

Prayer

*Lord,*
*in these Advent days,*
*you cry over,*
*landmine victims,*
*military deaths,*
*the sounds of mourning,*
*the flight of communities,*
*the shattering of lives.*

*So come to us*
*and overturn our tired ideas,*
*our violence,*
*our narrow judgements,*
*our human disconnections,*
*until your wisdom*
*invades*
*our understanding.*

Peter Millar

# DECEMBER 8

The Second Coming

*Righteousness shall be the belt around his waist,*
*and faithfulness the belt around his loins.*

*The wolf shall live with the lamb, the leopard shall lie down with the kid,*
*the calf and the lion and the fatling together,*
*and a little child shall lead them.*
*The cow and the bear shall graze,*
*their young shall lie down together;*
*and the lion shall eat straw like the ox.*
*The nursing child shall play over the hole of the asp,*
*and the weaned child shall put its hand on the adder's den.*
*They will not hurt or destroy on all my holy mountain;*
*for the earth will be full of the knowledge of the Lord*
*as the waters cover the sea.*

Isaiah 11:5–9

With Raymond Fung, of the Hong Kong Industrial Mission, and others, 600 factory workers in that colony, who had become Christians in the last four years, I worked on the interpretation within their own situation of the main doctrines of the Christian faith. Incarnation, crucifixion, resurrection, justification – these could be made recognisable realities, full of meaning in the Hong Kong industrial context. It was exciting to find old doctrines come alive within that very special context.

But one doctrine baffled them – the Second Coming. They found it hard to pray: 'Even so, come Lord Jesus.' In their experience, that had been a get-out for facing life and coping with it exactly as it is. Jesus would come and put everything right – so you need not be bothered about sufferings now, either of others or of yourself. How could those who hungered and thirsted for justice be content to sit passively under conditions as they existed and just wait for the return of Jesus Christ? In their Bible study periods, the factory workers came back again and again to the theme. But that doctrine seemed alien. It did not come alive, as the others did.

Then came a terrible industrial accident. Six workers, including a Christian, were killed. There was a mass funeral with 1000 people attending. Both the pastor and the chairman of the Communist trade union were given the opportunity to speak. The pastor spoke for an hour. His speech was divisive. He spoke of heaven and hell, the narrow and wide gates. Those who were of his kind and view would be saved, others would be lost.

The chairman of the Communist trade union spoke for only three or four minutes, but with great effectiveness. He pledged his union to fight for better legislation and better safety regulations; and ended with the Communist exhortation to the relatives to go on living courageously.

The Christian workers were furious. Here was a time to express solidarity in the human family and Christians had been divided off from unbelievers. An opportunity had been passed up of witnessing to Christ's justice and judgement and healing. Some of the new Christians met afterwards to give vent to their anger at the distortion of the gospel in the mouth of the pastor. One, in his indignation, blurted out, 'I wish Jesus had been here to speak for himself.'

At once, for many, the key turned in the lock of the doctrine of the Second Coming. The Christian group began to see how poorly they represented Christ on earth – not only the pastor, but all of them.

Ian M Fraser

Prayer

*Christ has no hands but our hands:*
*NO HANDS BUT OUR HANDS*
*TO DO GOD'S WORK IN THE WORLD.*

*Christ has no lips but our lips:*
*NO LIPS BUT OUR LIPS*
*TO PROCLAIM THE GOOD NEWS.*

*Christ has no love but our love:*
*NO LOVE BUT OUR LOVE TO SHARE*
*WITH THE IMPRISONED, THE SILENCED, THE PERSECUTED,*
*THE MARGINALISED. AMEN*

Responses from a service in Iona Abbey

# DECEMBER 9

*I was glad when they said to me, 'Let us go to the house of the Lord!'*
*Our feet are standing within your gates, O Jerusalem!*

Psalm 122:1

An Ecumenical Accompanier in East Jerusalem

'I'm sorry
I cannot offer you coffee
My house has just been demolished.'

We stand together
Family and supporter
Accompanied and Accompanier
The bulldozer drives away
The soldiers depart, laughing and joking

Leaving a pile of rubble
A storehouse of shattered memories
Here and there remembered objects –
The black T-shirt
The embroidered cushion
The Barbara Streisand CD

'They gave us ten minutes
Ten minutes to retrieve what we treasure most
The toys, the photographs, the keepsakes
We shall rebuild the house – *inshallah*
But some things we can never replace.'

'And why?
What did we do to harm them?
Why does the world allow them to hurt us so?
We do not hate the Israeli people
We do not understand them
All we want is peace – but peace with justice.'

I cannot answer their questions
I can do nothing but stand with them
Hold them
Weep with them

We stand together
Family and supporter
Accompanied and Accompanier

'I'm sorry
I cannot offer you coffee
My house has just been demolished.'

*The Arab peoples are well-known for their hospitality: it is impossible to visit a Palestinian home without being invited to have coffee or mint tea, and it is impolite to refuse. The sentence which forms the opening of this piece was actually said to two of my colleagues in the Jerusalem team minutes after they had stood with the family, watching as the bulldozer demolished their house with most of their possessions still inside. When I visited the site the next day, I saw in the rubble the T-shirt, cushion and CD referred to.*

Elizabeth Burroughs

Prayer

*Pray not for Arab or Jew,*
*for Palestinian or Israeli.*
*But pray rather for ourselves,*
*that we might not divide them in our prayers.*
*But keep them both together in our hearts.*
*Amen*

Source unknown

# DECEMBER 10

Being on the watchtower

*I shall stand at my post, I shall take up my position on the watchtower, keeping a look-out to learn what the Lord says to me.*

Habakkuk 2:1

I remember a friend saying to me that in uncertain times often the only thing we can do is to wait and to be watchful. It is a great insight. It reminds me of that other saying: 'In a dark time, the eye sees.' Often more clearly than in calmer times, I think.

And for Habakkuk, positioned on the watchtower, it was a time to keep faithful and to listen for the Lord's words. So it is with Advent. A time of watching: of waiting; of listening: of being still before the Sustainer and Creator of all. Surrendering our life to the creative action of Love and to the gift of God's grace in our hearts.

In the course of one month, through its daily prayers, the Iona Community remembers all the nations on earth. A few countries are prayed for on each day. And as we hear the names of the countries we can pray for specific events or situations in them. It is a daily spiritual exercise which keeps the mind globally alert. Some countries we may know little about, but we hold them and their peoples in prayer before the One who holds the whole world in His hands. In other words, as I understand it, we place that country into God's embrace for another day.

That kind of praying is rooted in an openness to God's guidance. It is not merely about us or our own ideas. In a sense, it's being on the watchtower – aware that all around is a world permeated and sustained by God's healing and hope. But also a world which is a witness to conflict, grinding poverty and unimaginable disconnection, as well as to beauty, laughter and extraordinary signs of compassion.

As we prepare to once again celebrate the birth of Jesus, may we seek from God's goodness a heart which is open to the world in all of its contradiction and possibility. To recognise the sacredness of ordinary life in fresh ways. Or in the wonderfully insightful words of the poet Les Murray: *the ordinary mail of the otherworld, wholly common, not postmarked divine …*

Prayer

*Renewing Christ,*
*let us dream. Let us be watchful.*
*Let us see visions of love, peace and justice.*
*Let us see healing of your earth.*
*Let us affirm with joy, humility, faith and confidence,*
*that you are –*
*the Life of the world!*

Peter Millar

# DECEMBER 11

The heartbeat of the gospel

*Blessed is that slave whom his master will find at work when he arrives.*

Luke 12:43

On one occasion, I mentioned to George MacLeod how often Jesus Christ warned those who had ears to hear, to wait, alert to developments. He waved the thought away with 'That is hardly at the heart of the gospel.' Not the heart. But it is also important that the heartbeat of the gospel get full attention.

I discern behind the advice a profound theological observation. The Great Doer in earthly life is God. There is no handover to consecrated human beings. Servants of God's purposes are called to be co-workers with Jesus Christ through the Holy Spirit to enable God's will to be fulfilled. But they have to be alert to find what God is getting up to. Then they are to find at what points they are called to stay out (as Paul was in Asia, Bithynia and Mysia, till he and his companions reached Troas and the European mission could begin), and at what points to be prepared to be shouted in, and if the latter, what particular contribution to be expected to make. Whatever light comes to an individual needs to be tested in community (as in Acts 13:1–3) – and not a community of the like-minded, but of all sorts to check whether what is asked is really of the Holy Spirit.

The fact is that we do not know what our life is for, without the Holy Spirit revealing, stage by stage, how life is to be spent. We become truly ourselves when we are 'clothed upon' by Christ – his true nature fulfilling our given nature. Our life will be lived truly not by assessing our talents and matching them to opportunities. On that basis Paul could have evangelised in Asia, Bithynia and Mysia and missed Troas. We are not to invest life in enterprises just because they are good. Nor are we to hesitate forever at crossroads. Professor John Billie once asked us, in class, what should be done if we came to a fork in life's road issuing in two options which, after prayer and research, seemed equally compelling. We could not answer. He suggested that we toss a coin. If at the end of all forms of consideration both ways seem equally personally challenging, we can take either; God will know the choice of either option and turn it to good. At that point I thought of a cowboy hero in *The Rover* magazine. He came to a town where all the sheriffs who held office previously had been eliminated by bad men. The office was vacant, open to applications. He wondered if he should apply. He decided to toss a coin. If it came up heads he would put himself forward, if tails he would not. The thirteenth time that he tossed the coin it came up heads, so he took the job.

The essence, in biblical terms, is to wait till situations are ripe – wait, alert – to be able, through the leading of the Spirit, to respond as required.

Pictures used in the Bible are of watchtowers and watchmen. In the Book of Habakkuk (who takes God to task, as did Job, for mismanaging the world) there is awareness that the initiative is with God. 'I will keep watch to see what God will say to me' (2:1). The answer comes: 'There is still a vision for the appointed time. It speaks of the end and does not lie. If it seems to tarry, wait for it' (2:3). Isaiah, looking for the restoration of Jerusalem, also envisions watchmen posted on its walls. They are not only to take no rest, staying on the *qui vive*; they are also to pester God to take action 'until he makes Jerusalem a theme of praise throughout the world' (62:7).

To wait and watch has to go with active service. Inactive waiting is ruled out. In the New Testament the figure of a householder returning from an engagement at an unexpected hour is used to applaud servants or slaves who have remained watchful for that return, still getting on with their work. 'Blessed is that slave whom the master will find getting on with his work, when he arrives' (Luke 12:43). That chapter illustrates the point by imagining the master's attendance at a wedding feast. It also uses another favourite picture: the Son of Man coming like a thief in the night so that those waiting need to have their guard up, not be found sleeping.

The Incarnation came when the time was ripe. It caught some off guard. But some were alert. Christ still comes in unexpected ways. We need to be wakeful to respond.

Prayer

*O God, you have set before us a great hope*
*that your Kingdom will come on earth,*
*and have taught us to pray for its coming:*
*make us ready to thank you for the signs of its dawning,*
*and to work and pray for the perfect day*
*when your will shall be done on earth as it is in heaven.*
*Amen*

*From* Iona Abbey Worship Book

Ian M Fraser

# DECEMBER 12

*Awake sleeper, rise from the dead, and Christ will shine upon you.*

Ephesians 5:14

A few reflections to keep us awake!

God matters: God's world matters: We matter to God.
– Seen on a poster

We must make no important decision without opening our hearts to love.
– Ignatius Loyola

God respects me when I work, but loves me when I sing.
– Rabindranath Tagore

Do all the good you can,
by all the means you can,
in all the ways you can,
in all the places you can,
to all the people you can,
as long as ever you can.
– John Wesley

Our lives begin to end the day we become silent about things that matter.
– Martin Luther King

God has lit up some lamp in my heart that nothing can put out.
– Indian saying

A zigzag path gets us there in the end.
– Seen on a poster

Every moment can be the small door through which the Messiah may enter.
– Jewish saying

It is central to belief in Jesus that we can still sing praises to God even in the darkest night.
– Christian de Cheyne of Algeria, 20th-century Christian martyr

God is: He is in Jesus so there's hope.
God is: He is here for us so it is worth it.
– David Jenkins

The great enemy of spiritual progress is the belief that you know it all already.
– Thuskey Rinpoche

If you are not on the edge then you have too much room.
– Seen on a poster

May the rains fall on our fields, the cows grow fat, and the children take the wisdom of the ancestors. May time stand still as we gaze upon the beauty that is around us, and may the love in our hearts envelope all those whom we touch.
– Zulu prayer

Peter Millar

Awake out of sleep

It is high time to awake out of sleep;
for our salvation is nearer at hand than when first we believed.

We confess that we sleep
when we think the world is as it always was.
It is high time to awake
to the truth that Jesus has come.
His summons is urgent in our midst.
Nearer than we know He is coming in judgement.
He might come in judgement this Christmas.

We confess that we sleep
when we think that power is still of this world.
It is high time to awake
to the truth that His power alone is working permanently.
All the civilisations builded in scorn of His power
are as if they had never been.
And our civilisation with them will equally go down.
Nearer than we know
He will be seen coming in power.
He might come in power this Christmas.

We confess that we sleep
when we think that His glory is veiled.
He has been seen,
He has died,
He has risen,

He reigns.

It is high time to awake to the truth
that His glory is manifest.
In all the deeds that sweeten,
in all the thoughts that help.
Nearer than we know
He will be seen coming in glory,
to exalt the humble and meek
and to cast down the mighty from their seats.
He might come in glory this Christmas.

And we ... we accept the ways of this world and its judgements.
We accept the powers of this world despite their obvious bankruptcy.
We accept the tinsel, the gold and the glare
despite their emptiness –
till with this world's eyes
we see Christmas coming as a carnival,
and not as a confusion of face.

Give us grace to wait in spiritual expectancy
His coming again to practise true humility;
to be exercised in the ways of real power,
to express His glory:
that we may recognise the kingship of a cradle,
the royalty of being ruled,
the seniority of service:
So that should He come this Christmas,
we would be found among those who worshipped

and not among those who would kill.
If these things would be:
it is high time to awake out of sleep.
His body bloody but His head crowned,

George MacLeod, Founder of the Iona Community

# DECEMBER 13

Five and five

*'At that time the Kingdom of Heaven will be like this. Once there were ten young women who took their oil lamps and went out to meet the bridegroom. Five of them were foolish, and the other five were wise. The foolish ones took their lamps but did not take any extra oil with them, while the wise ones took containers full of oil for their lamps. The bridegroom was late in coming, so they began to nod and fall asleep. It was already midnight when the cry rang out, "Here is the bridegroom! Come and meet him!" The ten young women woke up and trimmed their lamps. Then the foolish ones said to the wise ones, "Let us have some of your oil, because our lamps are going out." "No, indeed," the wise ones answered, "there is not enough for you and for us. Go to the shop and buy some for yourselves." So the foolish ones went off to buy some oil; and while they were gone, the bridegroom arrived. The five who were ready went in with him to the wedding feast, and the door was closed. Later the others arrived. "Sir, sir! Let us in!" they cried out. "Certainly not! I don't know you," the bridegroom answered.' And Jesus concluded, 'Watch out, then, because you do not know the day or the hour.'*

Matthew 25:1–13

Jesus told many stories
and if this is one of his,
which I doubt
(it feels more like an Early Church construction to me),
it's a strange one.

I remember bits of it from Sunday school –
they called it 'The five wise
and the five foolish virgins'
(virgins, you understand, meant young women).
The emphasis
was on being prepared
(the Guides and Scouts were on the right lines then)
on being good and helpful,
because
*God is always watching you*
*and you need to be ready*
*to come running*
*when he calls.*

My dad
was strong
on the next story in the Bible,
about using your talents –
all good Protestant work ethic stuff:
*You've been given gifts and opportunities,*
*don't waste them,*
*ability brings responsibility,*
*always do your best.*

The Methodism I grew up in
emphasised
the last story in the chapter,
the sheep and goats one:
*Act justly*

*care for those who need your help.*
*When you do that*
*you live for God.*

So when I come back to this story
as an adult
I come not only with life's experience,
but also with layers of memory
and messages from childhood,
which are part of who I am.

What hits me first
is the selfishness of the wise young women,
whose oil (according to many translators)
might well have enabled
all the lamps to burn brightly –
but they weren't willing
to risk sharing it
and kept it for themselves.

And who, I ask, is this arrogant bridegroom,
who arrives hours late
and excludes those
who are disadvantaged
by his behaviour?

Experience prompts me to ask the question:
Whose voice is missing from this story?
The bride –
how did she feel

when some of the guests
were not allowed to come to her wedding?
Were they her friends, her family, her neighbours,
these women shut out in the dark?
Had her groom
consulted her
before he barred the door?

Theologically
what do I learn from this story?
That God favours those
who have enough time and money
to stock up on what they might need,
whilst those who live day to day
will no way make God's grade?

Or that
God is always waiting to catch us out,
and when he does
he'll pretend
he never knew us,
never loved us
never heard our prayers?

I think not!

I want to rewrite this story.

In my version
the bride is waiting

just inside the open door
for her guests,
and when they arrive
she gives them a hug
and welcomes them to the feast.

Her guests are a real mixed bunch:
rich and poor,
sad and happy,
homemakers and adventurers,
old and young.

The party goes on for hours,
and when the oil runs out
she asks her groom to go down to the shops
and get some more.

And he does.

And when all the lamps are lit
the couple make their promises
in the midst of their guests:

to care for each other
to risk loving
to act justly

and to welcome
the God of love
and of strangers
into their lives.

I don't think
they'll be teaching
my version in Sunday schools,
but it might make Jesus,
the guest of saints and sinners,
smile.

Prayer

*Jesus the storyteller,*
*it's a joy to listen to you;*
*to laugh and to cry,*
*to ask questions,*
*to be filled with sense and wonder.*

*Tell me your stories*
*all the nights and days of my life,*
*and let your words*
*come alive*
*and dance in me. Amen*

Ruth Burgess

# DECEMBER 14

Not merely about fine words

*Jesus answered, 'Whoever has two shirts must give one to the person who has none, and whoever has food must share it.'*

Luke 3:11

This injunction of John the Baptist is part of a longer Advent reading (Luke 3:7–18) which contains many other suggestions for living in the way of God. John was powerful in his message when he asked people to 'turn away from their sins' but that turning was always linked to our everyday behaviour. His message, as he prepared the way for Jesus, was not merely about fine words. If we are to change – under God's guidance – then what we do with our lives each day matters. Matters to God and to others.

Some years back when I was living in Gugulethu, a township near Capetown in South Africa, I was struck all the time by the ways in which local folk faced up to their multiple sufferings. These words of John about giving your shirt and sharing your food jumped right off the pages of the Bible and into the streets of Gugulethu, despite its sufferings, violence and poverty. There human love had many faces, as did AIDS, which affected many local families.

I vividly remember chatting with a local, older woman, herself a poor person, who over many years had taken into her home children orphaned by AIDS. To visit that home was to be in the presence of living compassion. It was a small, simple home on a crowded street, yet in it one met Jesus. This wonderful woman had done far, far more than share her food and clothing. She had given her life, her few possessions, her love, her laughter and her wisdom to these kids who had nothing.

And when we encounter such selfless love, it becomes clear what John the Baptist meant as he spoke to the crowds on the banks of the River Jordan – a place which today witnesses much human suffering. The people were asking him how they could walk in God's way and turn back from their failures. 'What are we to do, then?' they asked the prophet. He answered, 'Whoever has two shirts must give one to the person who has none, and whoever has food must share it.'

That friend in Gugulethu, in her own tender way, invites us all to heed these words and to discover what really matters in the human soul. And in these days of Advent, we too can pause, and ask God to grant us hearts of deeper sharing, for we all know that we have much to give and, for some of us at least, not so much time left to do the giving!

Prayer

*Two shirts, Lord,*
*no, actually six –*
*and a fridge stocked with food*
*and much, much more besides.*
*So are you surprised I am sometimes burdened*
*and not free as you would like me to be?*

Peter Millar

# DECEMBER 15

Signs of hope

*The light shines in the darkness, and the darkness did not overcome it.*

John 1:5

*In the 2004 Gandhi Foundation International Peace Award lecture, Iona Community member Helen Steven said:*

'... I believe passionately in the power of non-violence. In times of great despair, it offers a way of courage, great companionship, immense potential for change, and above all, hope. Because there are signs of hope in the midst of our despair. 23 million people in Europe marching – many for the first time – against the war in Iraq; the steady quiet determined bravery of the Women in Black; volunteers pouring into Palestine to help with the olive harvest; in Trident Ploughshares seeing committed young people taking over the boring administrative jobs and not just the glamorous ones; the internet humming with activity and preparations for the G8; and on our own doorstep in the far north of Scotland, an enthusiastic group of local people planning a community buyout of Suilven, one of our most beautiful mountains, from a mighty landowner ...'

*Meditate on some signs of hope in your life*
*and in the life of the world ...*

A prayer from Noma-lady, Gugulethu, South Africa

*I have always found the following prayer/psalm, from Peter Millar's* Gugulethu Journal, *incredibly powerful and moving: a prayer of hope that rises out of an experience of crucifixion. When I read this prayer, I am always reminded that I am a rich, white Western man of such spiritual poverty. (Neil Paynter)*

From *A Gugulethu Journal*:

… Last week at one of the HIV/AIDS support group meetings, a local woman called Noma-lady, who is facing many hurdles rooted in poverty and weakness of body, wrote this prayer in her own language, Xhosa. Spiwo Xapile, the minister here, has translated it for me. I invite you to read Noma-lady's words slowly, and to walk with her and many others as a sister or brother. We belong together …

Prayer

God is love to me, and God is amazing even though I am not strong physically in terms of my health. Even though things are difficult I continue to go down on my knees and pray, and from time to time I see God responding to my prayer. I don't know how I could praise God's name in a way that is befitting God's greatness. I do not have the instruments appropriate enough to make the music that would truly express how I feel about God. There are times when I have sleepless nights and watch TV till morning, but I always feel comfort when I go on my knees and pray. I am sometimes up at 3am trying to sleep on that side or the other. There are times when the pain is so heavy; my hand with cramps: my fingers twisting. Had I not been connected with God I would be accusing people of causing this pain, but earlier in my life I chose a close relationship with God, though I am poor. God is with me in the morning when I wake up: God is around during sleep, and is with me as I try to walk around. I just cry knowing that God has heard my prayer. I live with great hope. Amen

Noma-lady

# DECEMBER 16

The pig ankle jig

*Yet for us there is one God, the Father, from whom are all things and for whom we exist, and one Lord, Jesus Christ, through whom are all things and through whom we exist.*

1 Corinthians 8:6

There's a guest concert at the MacLeod Centre on Iona each week; a sort of talent show. Guests of the Mac and Abbey come together and read poems, sing silly songs, put on little skits and plays …

One week, a serious classical musician got up, and played the first movement of Mendelssohn's violin concerto! … Afterwards, she told us about a dream she had had … A dream of hearing 'the music of the spheres'. And before lifting her violin to play us the music of the spheres, she described to us her dream first: her dream about seeing God, and a glorious vision of heaven …

Like an airport, she said. With souls coming up behind the glass like when you're standing waiting for new arrivals. Customs officials – the lesser saints. There was a party going on – Saint Julian welcomed her – took her burden, then handed her something to drink. Something gingery with stars in it; there were so many souls. There was a little gold cross lying on a table, and suddenly she turned and caught a glimpse of God from the back: a little wispy man with spiky white hair and purple Doc Martens. With a gold lamé cloak like Elvis, like Elvis wore. They were playing his favourite song and he was doing his dance.

'And this,' the serious, straight-faced woman said, 'is God's favourite song.' And she started to play – 'The pig ankle jig'. Joyfully. Gracefully. Beautifully. With her eyes closed. And everyone in the Mac started to clap, and cheer and laugh, and I heard God laughing too – flinging out the whole universe and having a jolly old time – and then we all went over to the commitment service in the Abbey.

On the way over, I could hear the pig ankle jig; could see it: in the way people walked and laughed together, in the jiggy way the elements danced around – in waves, sky, wind whipping up.

At the service I prayed, and made a commitment to listen and look for God dancing.

*What's your vision of God, Jesus's father?*

*Is he a stern, judgemental man*
*with his finger poised on the button of doom?*
*Or is he more a little wispy man with spiky white hair*
*and purple Doc Martens?*

*Does he enjoy sitting and listening to stiff hymns?*
*Or dancing to music like the pig ankle jig?*

*What's your vision of God the Father?*
*What's your vision of God? …*

Neil Paynter

# DECEMBER 17

Enlightenment and not explosion

*By the tender mercy of our God, the dawn from on high will break upon us, to give light to those who sit in darkness and in the shadow of death, to guide our feet into the way of peace.*

Luke 1:78–79

In *Chasing the Wild Goose: the Story of the Iona Community* by Ron Ferguson, Ron writes that when George MacLeod first saw the statue 'The Descent of the Spirit' by Jacob Lipchitz, which stands in the Cloisters of Iona Abbey, 'he saw the lineaments of an atomic bomb'. (Ed.)

*The Incarnation was indeed an inherent explosion into matter, setting up a chain reaction of igniting love that has sparked from heart to heart from that day to this and that one day will consume mankind in its lightsomeness or burning. The Celts called Christ 'the Sun behind all suns'. Ours is the first generation of mankind to know, not just upon our pulses but in our very textbooks, that there is no such thing as dead matter. The very atom is best described as light-energy. And has not the Church taught down the centuries that Christ is the Light of the World and its Life (energy)?*

*If we reduce such phrases to the concept of a flickering candle in the dark, or merely a mystic spark within the soul, if we miss the 'many-splendoured thing', then quite simply we have mislaid the key for which the modern world is blindly groping. Men will look elsewhere – and vainly – for their salvation. We stand, if we care to enter, on the edge of the most spiritual age the world has ever known.*

*Full acceptance of the Incarnation is the primary key to this atom as enlighten-ment and not explosion.*

George MacLeod

*O God, lead us from death to life,*
*from falsehood to truth.*
*Lead us from despair to hope,*
*from fear to trust.*
*Lead us from hate to love,*
*from war to peace.*
*Let peace fill our hearts,*
*our world, our universe.*
*Amen*

Universal prayer for peace

# DECEMBER 18

*'Come, let us go up to the mountain of the Lord, to the house of the God of Jacob;*
*that he may teach us his ways and that we may walk in his paths.'*
*For out of Zion shall go forth instruction,*
*and the word of the Lord from Jerusalem.*
*He shall judge between nations and shall arbitrate for many peoples;*
*they shall beat their swords into ploughshares,*
*and their spears into pruning hooks;*
*nation shall not lift up sword against nation,*
*neither shall they learn war any more.*

Isaiah 2:3–4

The map of non-violence, *from a talk*

… It is time for all people of goodwill to embrace a different way – the way of active, and proactive, non-violence. Instead of pre-emptive strikes, we need pre-emptive peacemaking. Not peace liking or peace wishing but peacemaking. Primarily, this means diplomacy, negotiation, listening, massive investment in conflict resolution, mediation and a wider vision. Above all, it means much more serious engagement with what it means to live with difference, with the recognition that people are different and will remain different. And it also therefore requires that non-violent action for justice and human rights and dignity is accelerated.

So what does it mean to attempt to live by the map of active non-violence? I believe that it is an invitation to live hopefully and to bear witness. David Stevens, the Leader of the Corrymeela Community in Northern Ireland, writes: *Jesus had a profound understanding of conflict and violence and his teaching should not be understood as impractical idealism. Instead it should be seen as a way of getting out of the reciprocity of conflict. Going the second mile, turning the other cheek, giving your cloak to the one who takes your coat (Matt 5:38–42) are all ways of doing the unexpected – the non-imitative thing which offers the possibility of breaking the reciprocity of conflict. Some translations of verse 39 speak of offering 'the wicked no resistance' or some such. A better translation is 'Don't react violently against the one who is evil' (the Scholars Version). What we are being challenged to do is not to resist evil but to find a creative way out of the reciprocity of action and reaction (an eye for an eye and a tooth for a tooth).*[1]

The Japanese-American theologian Kosuke Koyama writes:

*What is love if it remains invisible, inaudible, intangible. 'Those who do not love a brother or sister whom they have seen, cannot love God whom they have not seen.' The devastating poverty in which millions of children live is visible. Racism is visible. Machine guns are visible. Slums are visible. Starved bodies are visible. The gap between the rich and the poor is glaringly visible. Our response to these realities must be visible. Grace cannot function in a world of invisibility. Yet in our world, the rulers try to make invisible the alien, the orphan, the hungry and thirsty, the sick and imprisoned. This is violence. Their bodies must remain visible. There is a connection between invisibility and violence. People, because of the image of God they embody, must remain seen. Faith, hope and love are not vital except in what is seen. Religion seems to raise up the invisible and despise what is visible. But it is the 'see, hear, touch' gospel that can nurture the hope which is free from deception.*[2]

This connection between invisibility and violence is particularly strongly evidenced in war: I think particularly of the refusal of the 'coalition of the willing' to count the Iraqi dead, of the secrecy around Guantánamo Bay, around extraordinary rendition. But, 'people must remain seen'. To live hopefully, to bear witness, means to make the violence done to people visible; to say what we have seen, to ask what is still unseen, to break the culture of silence and to name names. There are, of course, many ways to do this; through campaigns and lobbying and advocacy. Sometimes it is simply to draw attention by presence; like the Mothers of the Disappeared in Argentina, or the Women in Black in many places. When members of the Iona Community sit down outside Faslane, we do not think that blockading is going to close the base then and there. We do it to make visible once again the huge capacity for death and destruction contained in every Trident submarine. It is what Ecumenical Accompaniers and Christian Peacemaker Teams do in the West Bank and Gaza.

But bearing witness is about more than just making violence visible. Here is David Stevens again: (Christians) are called to make this reconciliation visible – visible in terms of a quality of relationships, visible in terms of openness and hospitality. It is a visibility which serves the same purpose as Christ's visibility, namely, to reveal God and God's reconciling love. This is true holiness and is the ministry of reconciliation.[3] Bearing witness is also about making reconciliation visible, about making alternatives visible.

I spoke earlier about my interpretive key being spiritually-based and depending on a community. I have been part of the Iona Community all my life, first as a child of members, then as a member myself. Peacemaking and opposition to militarisation has been a central part of the Iona Community since its beginning in 1938. Our Founder, George MacLeod, who had enlisted at the age of 19, and who had been awarded the Military Cross and the

Croix de Guerre in the trenches of the First World War, and subsequently became a pacifist and socialist, had a holistic theology that did not just express itself in rebuilding on Iona, but in radical non-violence and sustained opposition to nuclear weapons and the arms trade.

This commitment to non-violence is expressed in the Community's Justice and Peace Commitment, which is one part of the fivefold Rule of faith and life to which all members adhere. Its first article states:

*We believe that the Gospel commands us to seek peace founded on justice and that costly reconciliation is at the heart of the Gospel.*

This is what I believe, and what I try to practise. But I know that if I was trying to do it alone, I would have given up a long time ago. Jesus's way of non-violence invites us to discover not just what we are against, but what we are for. It invites us to fullness of life. But fullness of life is not to be identified with having it all, or thinking we can. It requires a recognition that this fullness encompasses emptiness, that gain incorporates loss, that joy involves sorrow, that living means learning to let go, and to face death. All of this is so counter-cultural that I think it's almost impossible to follow the way of non-violence without a community. The spiritual base and nurture that the community I am part of offers crucial things:

- In the human search for meaning, the freedom to ask questions; it is in the struggle to name and articulate our truth that we learn to know ourselves, including our own capacity for violence

- In the human search for intimacy, the **creation of safe space** – accepting, non-judgemental, encouraging, disciplined – in which to know and be known

- In the human search for belonging, the **encouragement of the art of sharing** through a revaluing of the communal joys and a rebuilding of confidence in relationship

There is another set of principles which are important to members of the Iona Community, who share them with millions across the world. These are the principles of non-violence, developed out of many violent situations as comprising:

- respect for the opponent as a fellow human being

- care for everyone involved in a conflict

- refusal to harm, damage or degrade people/living things/the earth

- if suffering is inevitable, the readiness to take it upon oneself rather than inflict it on others; not retaliating to violence with violence

- belief that everyone is capable of change

- appeal to the humanity of the opponent

- recognition that no one has a monopoly of truth, so trying to bring together different truths

- belief that the means are the ends in the making, so the means have to be consistent with the ends

- openness rather than secrecy

Inadequately, and failing constantly, these are nevertheless what we seek to live by. They are, after all, an invitation to personal responsibility for the sake of a larger peace …

Kathy Galloway, from 'A Religious Perspective on Peacemaking'

Footnotes

1. *From* The Place Called Reconciliation: Texts to Explore, *David Stevens, The Corrymeela Press, 2008*

2. *Kosuke Koyama, from an address given at the WCC General Assembly, Harare, 1998*

3. *David Stevens, from* The Land of Unlikeness: Explorations into Reconciliation, *The Columba Press, 2004*

Kathy Galloway

Sparks of Light

*At an Iona Community plenary in 2009, members got together in small groups to share their thoughts on peace and peacemaking. Here are some of the things they spoke about, and some voices (Ed.):*

The bully is made in God's image too

Look into their eyes

No peace without justice

Peace with justice will provide Shalom (life in all its abundance), but peace without justice will only deliver *eirene* (absence of war)

Loving the hell out of your enemy will bring real peace

Everyday 'quiet' peace witness beside campaigning in public

Peace has been taken over by the military!

Need to hear from the military

Prayer changes everything

Naming violence (Faslane, Aldermaston …) and imaging/showing alternatives

Action coming out of a place of well-being, rather than from a place of guilt or fear.

You can't make peace while you are being unpeaceful

How to translate your anger into passion for action?

Don't let the Powers ('Caesar', Bush, Blair) lull you into a sleep

'Sometimes I feel overwhelmed. There is so much to do! … But then I remember what St Paul said in Corinthians: We all have gifts. Some folk are good on the barricades, some are good at writing letters … We can't do everything: We are all pieces of the jigsaw … We are all sparks of Light …'

I will seek peace

I will seek peace at heart
Try to overcome my fears, my anxieties and troubled, anxious mind
I will look for solace
Search for comfort
I will seek peace at heart

I will seek peace at home
Reach out to those who are victims of abuse
   through age or gender or sexuality
I will challenge those who are perpetrators
Speak up for those who have no voice
I will seek peace at home

I will seek peace in the virtual world
Encourage young and old to dream the right dreams
live creatively, have real adventures –
which are free from violence or aggression
I will seek peace in the virtual world

I will seek peace with the earth
I'll campaign for the forests
Buy fairtrade products, recycle, keep a compost
and wonder at the beauty of nature
I will seek peace with the earth

I will seek peace in the marketplace
Live humbly and responsibly
Share my wealth and my home

Stand up for the rights of the poor and exploited
I will seek peace in the marketplace

I will seek peace not war
Study non-violence, resolve conflict,
campaign against arms, lobby governments
and challenge apathy
I will seek peace not war

And in my seeking
I will live with hope
Strive for change
Act with humility … courage … and faith
And choose love not hate …

Neil Squires, written for worship at an Iona Community plenary; reflecting on themes from the World Council of Churches' 'Decade to Overcome Violence'

# DECEMBER 19

Child at heart

*Truly I tell you, whoever does not receive the kingdom of God as a little child will never enter it.*

Luke 18:17

At one time, I taught English as a second language to adults and children. One afternoon (when we were covering verbs, I think), I wrote this on the blackboard for the children to fill in with whatever words they liked:

SOMETIMES I'M HAPPY _____.

One Christmastime, years later (when I was working as a nurse's aide with the elderly), I asked a lively 98-year-old woman, whom I was sitting with at lunchtime feeding, the secret of a long life …

'A glass of sherry before bed,' she answered, and I laughed … 'Believe it or not,' she said seriously … 'I still feel like a child at heart …… Otherwise, it's hopeless,' she added, after a long silence. It suddenly felt like it was *she* who was feeding me.

Like the 98-year-old woman in the nursing home, I still feel like a child at heart. Sometimes in an immature way – I feel insecure, scared, needy … But at other times, I feel a childlike sense of wonder, and joy; and I'm suddenly able to be silly, to laugh, to dance. And it feels like a healing flood of God's infinite grace.

Neil Paynter

Sometimes I'm happy

*Sometimes I'm happy in the summertime blue*
*Sometimes I'm happy talking to you*

*Sometimes I'm happy dancing the spin-around-dizzy*
*Sometimes I'm happy sitting still in the busy*

*Sometimes I'm happy waving to train people*
*Sometimes I'm happy leaping*
*my mind off the steeple*

*Sometimes I'm happy*
*playing my harmonica*
*(but my dog isn't)*

*Sometimes I'm happy wearing my straw hat all day*
*Sometimes I'm happy watching my cat at play*
*(or watching my cat*
*knead and purr,*
*knead and purr the comforter)*

*Sometimes I'm happy talking to cows*
*Sometimes I'm happy taking I'm-the-most-famous bows*

*Sometimes I'm happy eating macaroni and chocolate sauce*

*Sometimes I'm happy using the good cups for tea*
*Sometimes I'm happy making up a song that goes Tra la la lee*
*(bum de bum)*

*Sometimes I'm happy grabbing Babshe's ears*
*Sometimes I'm so happy I'm in tears*

*Sometimes I'm happy swinging my self*

*Sometimes I'm happy running where I wanna get*
*Sometimes I'm happy meeting someone new I've never met*

*Sometimes I'm happy seeing bottom – then a fish*
*Sometimes I'm happy squishing and stirring*
*ice cream in a dish*

*Sometimes I'm happy seeing something very small*
*(like a tiny red spider)*

*Sometimes I'm happy saying favourite words like 'mariposa'*

*Sometimes I'm happy collecting stuff*
*(like shells and rocks and coins,*
*and house and car keys people lost in grassy fields*
*and car lots)*

*Sometimes I'm happy how the way geese fly and honk*
*Sometimes I'm happy hearing a banjo*
*plink*
         *plank*
*plunk …*
*flaillll111*

*Sometimes I'm happy for no reason at all –*
*and I think that's the happiest happy of all*

A class of children and their teacher

# DECEMBER 20

Snow scene

*In his hand are the depths of the earth;*
*the heights of the mountains are his also.*
*The sea is his, for he made it;*
*and the dry land, which his hands have formed.*

Psalm 95:4–5

When I was a child in Canada I thought it was snowing all over the world at Christmastime. In Canada, in China, in Africa … I knew it was hot in Africa – I just thought the snow melted faster there.

When I was a child, I used to think that everyone lived like I did: had snow at Christmastime, a mother and father, brothers, sisters, a dog or a cat, Kentucky Fried Chicken for dinner on Friday nights, a ten-speed bike …

Somewhere along the line I realised I lived in an illusion.

I remember one Christmas, getting a 'snow scene' in my stocking: One of those globes you shook – and it snowed inside. It was an old-fashioned street scene of a little boy in a brown coat and cap, standing underneath a street lamp. You could just shake it up and watch the snow flurry down upon the town and the boy – then do it again. It was magical. I couldn't put it down.

I found it in a box as a teenager. I thought the figure was me as a child: stuck inside a world of illusion. Around that time I had started to get involved in volunteer work at a downtown drop-in centre and to read more about the outside world: about things like the Sandinista Revolution in Nicaragua, the American bombing of Vietnam and Cambodia and life under the Khmer Rouge, the Socialist world revolution, Gandhi's Soul Force … I was dying to break out. My dream was to travel and work overseas …

At Christmas time, I often think about people I know in other countries: Folk I met while travelling and working. Friends I made on Iona …

I think of Jimmy, whom I met when I was working in a Simon Community night shelter in King's Cross. Jimmy was seventeen years old and *loved* music – Led Zeppelin, Pink Floyd, The Clash … We talked for nights and nights about just music, and the liberation of it, before he ever told me anything about the violent life he had escaped. I often wonder if he ever moved off the streets and into his own flat with his own stereo, which was his dream. I wonder if he ever learned how to play the lead to 'Communication Breakdown' on electric guitar, which was his fantasy.

I think of a woman whom I met on a bench in a leafy park in Sarajevo, just before the Balkan wars erupted: she was wrapped in a ragged bandage of clothes and her hands and legs were swollen. I shared my bread and cheese with her. We couldn't really carry on a conversation, but from the way she waved her bandaged hands, and from the way her grey, seer's eyes searched the bruised skies, I could understand something was in the air. I often wonder if she lived through the bombings …

I think of Robert, whom I met on Iona, whose family owed a farm in Mugabe's Zimbabwe …

I think of Felicia and Mercy*, who I last heard were living in a refugee camp in Uganda ...

*Think of folk you know in other countries, or who live far away. Pray for their safety and peace ...*

*Pray for organisations working to bring security, development, hope to communities across the world.* NGOs like Oxfam, Save the Children, Médecins San Frontières, Christian Aid ... *Give a donation to one of these organisations this Christmas.*

*Pray for writers and editors working to communicate a deeper, more inclusive worldview than that broadcast by the corporate news machine and revealed in the tabloids. Publications like* The New Internationalist, Resurgence, Hospitality: the Newspaper of the Open Door Community ... *Take out a subscription to one of these alternative sources of news and inspiration, or give a gift subscription to a friend – spread the word.*

Prayer

*Baby Jesus, shake us up;*
*help us to break out of this Western world of illusion*
*we are trapped in and*
*entranced by.*

*Free our hands*
*to do your work.*

Neil Paynter

* See reading for November 30

# DECEMBER 21

That place where we are truly ourselves

*How wonderful it is to see a messenger coming across the mountains, bringing good news, the news of peace! He announces victory and says to Zion, 'Your God is king!' Those who guard the city are shouting, shouting together for joy! They can see with their own eyes the return of the Lord to Zion. Break into shouts of joy, you ruins of Jerusalem! The Lord will rescue his city and comfort his people. The Lord will use his holy power: he will save his people, and all the world will see it.*

Isaiah 52:7–10

This is the 'great summons' to the people of Israel firstly to 'hear' and then to 'awake'. It's the long-awaited news that the Kingdom of God is at hand, and the message is to be heard by all who actively pursue righteousness. By those who long for deliverance. As one commentator puts it so beautifully: 'There is to be a new beginning for God's wounded people on the yonder side of judgement!'

A fresh start. And the messenger, or messengers, are welcomed with open arms and much rejoicing. God will rescue his people, and the nations will also shout for joy. And through it all a responsibility lies not only with the hoped-for leader but with all the people – that they would truly hear God's word and awake to its implications.

Each year in the service known as the Festival of Nine Lessons and Carols, sections of Isaiah are read. The prophet's words, although rooted in a different social and historical context, are, in the hearts of believers, inextricably linked to the coming of Christ and to the good news of the Gospel. The news of liberation expressed in these words of Graham Kendrick, which are based in scripture:

*He comes the broken hearts to heal*
*the prisoners to free,*
*The deaf shall hear, the lame shall dance,*
*the blind shall see.*

On hearing these words when I was a kid, I used to think: *but I'm not blind, or deaf, or lame, or imprisoned, or carrying a broken heart.* Now I know better! Perhaps we all do as we become more aware of our own frailties, inner wounds and silent sorrows. Yet the more I recognise these realities in my own life, the more I understand the liberation and hope which Christ offers. John Newton, back in the 18th century, was experiencing this same new-found freedom in Christ when he wrote the great lines:

*Through many dangers, toils and snares*
*I have already come,*
*'tis grace has brought me safe thus far*
*and grace will lead me home.*

So we stop in the midst of our often frenetic lives and hear again the tender invitation of Christ to return 'home'. To come back, as many spiritual guides have taught us, to 'the Father's or Mother's heart'. To that place where we know both that God matters and that we matter to God. That place where we are truly ourselves because we are held in God.

Prayer

*Lord,*
*help me to stop in my tracks today –*
*even for 10 seconds –*
*and discover again*
*where my true home is:*
*that place in your love,*
*where I always belong.*

Peter Millar

# DECEMBER 22

David's conversion

*'Blessed are you among women, and blessed is the fruit of your womb.'*

Luke 1:42

I used to smoke a lot of weed … This was back in the days when I was feeling really depressed and stressed. Back in my early 20s. I'd dropped out of university and had no idea what to do with my life. I had a job in a video store: videos were big back then. I worked in the evenings, got home around midnight, and sat up and smoked weed and watched videos.

I smoked weed and watched movies all night, then crashed, and got up and went to work. The job wasn't hard, I didn't have to be too 'with it'. I'd spend all my time doing that. I thought about going back to school but had no money. And no ambition or direction anyway. I lived in a small apartment. Smoking weed took me away from thinking about my future, about my girlfriend, who'd broken up with me, and about some heavy-duty family problems I couldn't deal with then. It was an escape. Made me feel mellow and detached from things. I'd watch movies like *Star Wars* and *The Wall*. Or put music on my stereo sometimes, and listen to it in headphones, and get lost deep in a landscape …

One day I went out to meet my connection, who had a good regular supply of Columbian, but missed him somehow, and ended up in the middle of a sort of forest nearby. I was bugged. I glanced around the woods, and thought it would be a good place to come and smoke weed sometime. I sat in the forest, on this crumbling log … I heard the birds singing. Stared at the pattern of light and shade. I liked the space. It was sort of calming. I went back some days. Sometimes I brought weed along; sometimes I didn't.

The more I went there, the more it felt like *my* place. Not that I grew possessive of it, but I got to know it, explore it. As I did, I found myself thinking about myself less. I felt less lost in the forest of me; less trapped in the tangle of my problems. I saw different birds, and went home and looked them up in a book I'd bought. I went there in different seasons – saw the technicolour autumn, and in the springtime, the buds coming out; little red berries in wintertime, with the smell of spruce and pine. In the summer, I even picked some blueberries. There was something about being there. I felt more connected. Rooted.

One day I went, and saw some company starting to cut the woods down. I asked them what they were doing. 'Cutting the woods down to build more houses,' they said. 'You can't cut the woods down,' I said. 'Just watch us,' they said.

I was angry. I called up the local council. They said it was all decided; that the resolution was passed and I couldn't do anything about it. 'Call Greenpeace,' they said. So I did! I talked to someone at Greenpeace, and they sent me some information on the destruction and loss of green space in cities. They said I couldn't do much about the situation where I was living, but there were other things I *could* act on before it was too late. There were even worse situations: in Brazil the rainforests were being cut down and natives of the rainforests being uprooted or killed – a whole way of life vanishing and animals and healing plants becoming extinct. They said there was a talk about it at a community centre in town, so I went along. At the meeting they said they were looking for volunteers. So I volunteered.

I felt energised by the work. I found that working during the day, I didn't smoke as much weed. I met some nice people; made some friends.

I got to know a lot about the issues: I'd always liked reading. One day a job opened up at the office, and I applied and got it. I quit the video store and went to work for Greenpeace!

One time we had a weekend away. It was a staff bonding thing. There was a Native American elder who led the weekend. He spoke about our relationship to Mother Earth. In our job of protecting the earth we needed to nurture and deepen our connection with Mother Earth, he said. He spoke about the intricate wonder of the natural world, and the Great Spirit. He spoke about a lot of things I felt but had never put into words.

At the end of the weekend, he invited us all to take part in a ceremony where he burned sweet grass. Sweet grass was a gift of Mother Earth. 'The hair of Mother Earth.' We all came from Mother Earth, he said. It smelled a bit like weed, but nicer. He passed it around the circle. He said to fan the smoke over your heart … and over your mind … and over your body … I felt different after the ceremony. More whole somehow.

I find it funny sometimes: that I went looking for weed one day and ended up becoming an environmental campaigner. I've since gone back to university. I'm studying environmental law. It'll be a long road but I'll get there. I want to do everything I can to protect Mother Earth.

To support myself while I'm studying, I work on environmental documentaries: I do research, even write some scripts – so I guess all that experience in the video store and watching all those movies all night didn't go to a total waste!

Prayer

*Spirit of the living God,*
*enter us*
*body, mind and spirit*
*and heal us of all that harms us,*
*in the name of Jesus.*
*Amen*

*Prayer from the Iona Abbey Healing service (adapted)*

Neil Paynter

# DECEMBER 23

Timeless and completely contemporary

*Mary said, 'My heart praises the Lord: my soul is glad because of God, my Saviour, for he has remembered me his lowly servant!'*

Luke 1:46–48

These great words from Luke's account of Christ's birth, ring across the centuries. They are both timeless words, and completely contemporary. The words of a humble, unknown woman living right on the edge of the Roman Empire take us to the heart of our fragile humanity. And to the heart of God.

In his commentary on Luke, the New Testament scholar G.W.H. Lampe made the point that many of the words attributed to Mary in the Magnificat look back to the song of Hannah in the Book of Samuel, and to certain of the psalms. Mary's great song of hope and of praise, like much in this narrative, links the fulfilment of the Messianic hope of Israel with the original covenant promise to Abraham. The promise is being made sure, not through kings and emperors and people of power, but through a young woman who has never sought fame or made the headlines. She it is who carries the Messiah.

Every day as part of my prayer discipline as a member of the Iona Community, I repeat a version of the Magnificat written by Janet Morley, whose beautiful and powerful prayers are used in many countries. Janet's words are contemporary while remaining faithful to the biblical text. They take us into the guts of Mary's message for the modern world. A world in which many people – children, women and men – are far from free. Are in fact oppressed and violated and cast down. And yet, and yet, it is often they who teach us how to sing 'of the longing of God'. That's the miracle!

Peter Millar

*Sing out my soul, sing of the holiness of God;*
*who has delighted in a woman,*
*lifted up the poor, satisfied the hungry,*
*given voice to the silent, grounded the oppressor,*
*blessed the full-bellied with emptiness,*
*and with the gift of tears those who have never wept;*
*who has desired the darkness of the womb*
*and inhabited our flesh.*
*Sing of the longing of God. Sing out my soul.*

Janet Morley

# DECEMBER 24

Keep on dancing the samba

*I am the Lord, I have called you in righteousness,*
*I have taken you by the hand and kept you;*
*I have given you as a covenant to the people, a light to the nations,*
*to open the eyes that are blind,*
*to bring out the prisoners from the dungeon,*
*from prison those who sit in darkness.*

Isaiah 42:6–7

In my early twenties – as a part-time job while I was trying to finish my university degree – I taught English as a second language to refugees, asylum seekers and 'new Canadians' at the YMCA in Windsor, Ontario, Canada. It was an amazing job. I met so many amazing people – from Central America, South America, Vietnam, Eastern Europe … I wasn't exactly unworldly at the time, but meeting all these people really opened my eyes – and mind: I met a family who had taken to sea in a leaky boat with twenty others to escape government troops who had attacked their village; I met a man who had escaped a prisoner of war camp in Iran, and had walked over mountains and deserts in his bare feet; I met a woman who had fled guerrillas in Peru, not long after giving birth to her daughter, whom she carried through jungles and cities on her back. And I met Marco, who had been a labour leader in a factory in El Salvador, and had been arrested and tortured by the police – he was the most gentle, generous person. I couldn't understand how someone who had been so brutally, mercilessly tortured could still be so gentle and loving. I certainly wouldn't be, wasn't. I guessed he understood something about the fragility and preciousness of life.

I had a certain respect and status as a teacher: Government departments would contact me to enquire the progress of certain students; and sometimes I would write letters to colleges and schools for students so that they could get on training courses. It felt good to be able to help these new friends.

Sometimes we'd all go for coffee after class. One thing that amazed me was how active in Canadian life many of my students already were – in parent groups, tenant groups, credit unions – and how involved in life back home they remained. They had escaped horrific conditions, yet were in regular contact with not only family and friends but underground groups and organisations working for freedom and justice in their lands. I probably would have just wanted to leave the past behind; keep my head down – for the fates of many of my students were far from decided: some could still be, and likely were, sent back 'home'.

One Christmas, Marco invited me to a party at his community centre after midnight Mass – it was great. There was dancing and live music – a band with drums, guitars, flute, someone playing marimba. There were fold-up tables crowded with food – roast chicken, rice, potato salad – cold Mexican beer sweating in a big metal washbasin. The hall was so hot and cooking with music, dancing and conversation I forgot it was twenty below outside. For a moment I forgot I was in Canada.

There were children running around excitedly. I watched Marco, who had been tortured by death squads, dancing a samba. I watched him expertly move his feet that had been bastinadoed. *You can't chain down the human spirit,* I thought … His daughters were full of life. Over the passionate music, Rosanna told me that she wanted to study to be a doctor after high school. Maria said she wanted to be a school teacher. Their open smiles radiated spirit, and I thought of how lucky Canada was to have this family as citizens. They seemed hope and new life for a country that seemed to me, at the time – cold, hard, stiff, apathetic, individualistic; still white as snow in places.

Marco came over and gave me some rum to try. It had a hot sweet kick. He laughed, and we went out to watch the fireworks. Later, Maria tried to teach me how to dance the samba.

I received Christmas cards from the family for years after. Every Christmas it warmed my heart. In the last one I received, Rosanna was a doctor, and Maria was a nurse and was married – and had just had a baby girl. 'Thanks for being such a great teacher,' Marco wrote. 'And keep on dancing the samba!' he nudged and winked. I could hear his laugh and see his big smile.

Working as a teacher taught me about so many things – about world politics and people's liberation struggles, about different kinds of music, different foods – I learned new words, dances – I learned more in that time than I ever taught my students! One thing I learned was that there was a lot more to finding peace than finally getting my university degree.

*Pray for refugees and asylum seekers living in strange new countries. For all sent back to places of danger and death …*

*In the West, we are coming to a time of cutbacks. Right-wing governments and political parties are claiming that refugees and asylum seekers are a drain on countries' resources. The drain on our resources has been the arms trade, and the big banks: Military expenditure in the US in 2008 was 607 billion dollars; in the UK it was equivalent to 65.3 billion dollars (most recent SIPRI statistics). In 2009, people around the world gave failed banks, and failed bank CEOs, trillions of pounds.*

*Refugees bring great benefits – a richness of culture, and a wealth of energy, skills, new ideas and experience … To take action: www.refugeesinternational.org, www.refugeecouncil.org.uk*

Neil Paynter

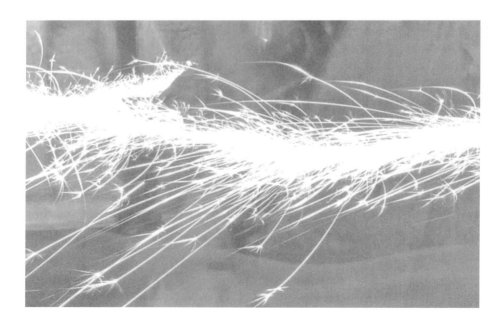

# CHRISTMAS EVE

Across this beautiful and complex world

*The kindness and generosity of God our Saviour has dawned upon the world.*

Titus 3:4

On our world! Our world in all of its myriad confusions and uncertainties, this kindness and generosity of God has dawned! And across this beautiful and complex world these gifts of God are given. Given to …

*those in positions of great power,*
*and those who have no power at all;*

*those who are rich beyond dreams,*
*and those who live in unimaginable poverty;*

*those who find faith in God difficult,*
*and those who don't;*

*those who know deep love,*
*and those who feel abandoned;*

*those who oppress others,*
*and those who work for justice;*

*those who lie on beds of pain,*
*and those who run marathons;*

*those who feel secure in themselves*

*and those who dread a new day dawning;*

*those who know all the answers,*
*and those who don't feel they have any;*

*those who live with hope,*
*and those who have lost it;*

*those who live in freedom,*
*and those who are chained;*

*those who celebrate a birth,*
*and those who journey into the mystery of death.*

*And thinking of them all, we wait, in hope, for Christmas morning.*

Peter Millar

# CHRISTMAS DAY

With the bullocks close by and the chickens running in and out

*I bring you good news, news of great joy for the whole nation. Today there has been born to you in the city of David a deliverer – the Messiah, the Lord.*

Luke: 2:10–11

*How silently, how silently,*
*the wondrous gift is given!*
*So God imparts to human hearts*
*the blessings of his heaven.*
*No ear may hear his coming;*
*but in this world of sin,*
*where meek souls will receive him, still*
*the dear Christ enters in.*

Phillips Brooks

For many years our home was in South India. Very early on Christmas morning, long before the sun was up over the palm trees and paddy fields, the village folk would be in church preparing for the Christmas services. It was still dark, but the sense of anticipation was palpable as they made beautiful their humble place of worship. By the time the service started, most of the congregation would be standing or sitting outside the small building, with its thatched roof and open sides, because the church itself was overflowing hours before the Christmas songs were sung. And I mean overflowing! Everyone in their Christmas clothes and garlands – the whole place a sea of colour, laughter and joy. With the bullocks close by and the chickens running in and out.

Above all it was the sense of anticipation and of excitement which made these Christmas mornings so memorable. Jesus was here! Alive in their midst. This was not a story from 2000 years earlier – this was reality here and now. It was the blessing of heaven present on earth.

As the rich sound of the Tamil Christmas lyrics moved through the village and held us and all the village's animals in a web of joy and light, it came home to me again that one thing was certain – that where humble souls were open to God, the dear Christ entered in. In this materially poor, but spiritually rich, place the faith of the local community was so evident. I will never forget the often wrinkled and knotted, expectant hands reaching out for the body and blood of Jesus – the One who gave them hope and healing, not just on Christmas morning, but every day. Their eyes were seeing Him, not in a stable in Bethlehem, but on the dusty, sun-drenched streets of an Indian village. And they knew deep in their souls, that despite everything that life would throw at them, the promise of God to his people was sure.

Prayer

*For a moment*
*on this Christmas Day*
*let me pause*
*and still my heart*
*and know*
*that You*
*have come to earth for me.*

Peter Millar

# A CHAIN REACTION OUT INTO ALL THE WORLD

'The need is a return to the Incarnation in modern terms. That is why we like the Lipchitz statue. A little like a bomb, but the Incarnation was an atomic explosion – a chain reaction out into all the world!

The Holy Spirit is the dove, the eyes wide open. The highest expression of nature is the woman. But the woman is blind, blind about the meaning of suffering. Animal creation is also blind, the lamb. Down comes the Holy Spirit to embrace and redeem the natural order … Sight comes to the world! The Lamb, the proverbial symbol of suffering, becomes the Lamb of God, the agent of the world's salvation …'

George MacLeod, from the film 'Sermon in Stone'
(Wild Goose Publications)

Photo of the Lipchitz statue in the Cloisters of Iona Abbey,
by David Coleman

Magnificat in bronze:
The story of the statue in the Cloisters of Iona Abbey

On Christmas Eve 1958, a ship sailing from Poland came down the west coast of Scotland, freighted with a unique cargo. On Christmas Day, the statue which in Iona Community circles is known as 'The Descent of the Spirit' was landed in Scotland, destined for Iona. It caused something of a stir at the time, since it is unmistakably a statue of the Virgin Mary. The legend on the reverse of the statue leaves no room for doubt. Composed by the sculptor himself, the words are in French and read 'Jacob Lipchitz, a Jew loyal to the faith of his ancestors, has made this Virgin, for good relations ('la bonne entente') among men on the earth, that the Spirit may reign.' I don't suppose the statue causes much furore today, but fifty years on, it seems a good time to tell its remarkable story, a story which, I believe, shows how that statue holds within itself issues which continue to disturb and challenge us.

A good place to begin the story is with the sculptor. Chaim Jacob Lipchitz was born into a Jewish family in 1891, in the town of Druskienniki, in Lithuania. From an early age, he drew and modelled in clay, and after school in Bialystok and Vilna, he went to Paris, arriving there in 1909. He became part of that extraordinary flowering of European art at the beginning of the 20th century, numbering among his close friends Chaim Soutine, Juan Gris and Amedeo Modigliani. In 1916 he married Berthe Kitrosser, a poet, and a wedding portrait of the couple by Modigliani hangs in the Art Institute of Chicago. In 1922, a Dr Albert Barnes visited the artist in Paris and commissioned work for his home at Merion, Pennsylvania (now the Barnes Foundation). So began a connection with the United States which was to prove decisive for the future.

Lipchitz became a French citizen in 1924, and began using 'Jacques' as a first name. All the while, his work was developing along 'cubist' lines, and in 1930, his first retrospective exhibition was held in Paris, while his work was shown for the first time in America, in New York, in 1935.

In 1940, German forces occupied Paris, and Lipchitz and Berthe fled to Toulouse. A year later, they sought asylum in the United States and escaped to New York, thanks to the contacts already in place. Not everyone was so fortunate. Between 1941 and 1944, some 74,000 Jews were deported from France, including French citizens, mostly to Auschwitz.

After the war, Lipchitz and Berthe returned to Paris in 1946, where they stayed for six months, before Lipchitz himself returned to New York. Berthe preferred to remain in Paris and they were divorced soon after. In 1948, Lipchitz married the sculptor Yulla Halberstadt and ten years later became an American citizen. Lipchitz died in 1973, on the island of Capri, and was buried in Jerusalem. His name is associated with other sculptors of the cubist style – Archipenko, Henri Laurens, Brancusi, Duchamp-Villon and Gonzales – and his work is represented widely across the United States and Europe. In a catalogue of his work which I've seen, the statue on Iona is the only one listed as being in the United Kingdom.

The statue in Iona has its genesis in that visit Lipchitz made to Paris in 1946. There, Lipchitz accepted a commission by a French priest, Father Couturier, to make a statue for the Baptistry of a new church which he was having built at Assy, in Haute-Savoie. Couturier was a Dominican priest, whose vision was the revitalisation of the Church through architecture and art.

What makes the church so remarkable is that Couturier wanted the most outstanding artists of the day to contribute to its decoration, irrespective of their religious affiliation or lack of it. As a result, the church contains work by Marc Chagall, Ferdinand Leger, Georges Rouault, Henri Matisse and many others, including Lipchitz. Lipchitz began work on the commission, back in New York, in 1949, but in 1952 a fire in his studio destroyed a number of works, including the commission for Assy. The statue was eventually completed in 1955 and was installed in that year in the church at Assy, where it stands today. And Lipchitz gave it a name. He called it: 'Notre Dame de Liesse'. 'Liesse' is a somewhat archaic French word which means 'jubilation'. Our statue on Iona is a second or third casting of that original work, and we are quite at liberty to give it any name we choose. But we should know that for the past 50 years, it's 'Our Lady of Jubilation' which has stood at the heart of the Cloisters in Iona Abbey.

That Lipchitz had made two further castings of the statue was the result of a commission given to him by a Mrs Jane Blaffer Owen, of Texas. Her vision was that one should stand in New Harmony, Indiana, and that the other should go to Iona. And the roots of that vision lie in her family history. Mrs Owen was in direct lineal descent through marriage from Robert Owen, the 19th-century social reformer, whose name is especially connected with New Lanark. Less well known, perhaps, are Owen's links with New Harmony.

Robert Owen was a Welshman, born in Newtown, in Montgomeryshire, in 1771. He lived for some years in Manchester as a young man, where he became a partner in a cotton-spinning firm. His involvement in that trade took him regularly to Glasgow, the city and the surrounding area growing at that time as an industrial centre. There he met David Dale, who had established his mills at New Lanark in 1785. Dale was a successful textile manufacturer, merchant, dyer and banker, but his health was failing and he was keen to sell. In 1799, Owen bought New Lanark, and in the same year married Dale's daughter, Caroline. In the New Lanark community, Owen began to put into practice reformist ideas which had been nurtured in his mind by his exposure to the debates and lectures of the Manchester Literary and Philosophical Society. Owen's concerns took him into issues of education, social and working environment, social welfare and cooperation, child labour, and religion, about which he was both sceptical and tolerant. At the same time, Owen was a very good businessman. New Lanark, as well as being a successful experiment in community, was also very profitable, and helped to make Owen a very wealthy man.

From 1812 onwards, Owen's ideas began to be more widely known and visitors made their way to New Lanark in ever-increasing numbers, including Americans. In this way, Owen heard about a community on the banks of the Wabash River, in Indiana. This community, called Harmonie, was founded by the Harmony Society, a group who had separated from the German Lutheran Church, under the leadership of Johann Georg Rapp. Known as Harmonists, they had settled first in Pennsylvania, and had gone to the Wabash in 1814. But now, Rapp was also keen to sell, and in 1824 Owen sailed to America, and the following year, bought New Harmony, as he then called it. His hope was to create on the Wabash at New Harmony a replica of the community he had developed on the Clyde at New Lanark. Things, however, did not work out that way, and in 1828, Owen sold off what remained of the community and returned to Britain. For the rest of his life, he campaigned tirelessly for social reform, and died, in 1858, in the town of his birth.

The connection with Mrs Owen of Texas has to do with the fact that Owen's sons and one of his daughters made their homes in America, making a significant contribution to American life. One of the sons, Robert Dale Owen, was left in charge at New Harmony, teaching in the school and working closely with the feminist Fanny Wright. In 1832 he was elected to the Indiana Legislature, and to the House of Representatives in 1845. During the Civil War, he was outspoken in his opposition to slavery and later wrote two books on the subject. Another son, David Dale Owen, established a laboratory at New Harmony which was the nucleus of what later became the US Geological Survey, his geological and natural science collections providing the beginnings of the Smithsonian Institute. This is the family into which Mrs Jane Blaffer Owen married.

The Lipchitz statue which Mrs Owen commissioned for New Harmony stands today in the centre of what is called 'The Roofless Church', a space for worship and meditation designed by the American architect Robert C. Johnson, and with an entranceway made by Lipchitz himself. And 100 years after Robert Owen's death, the other statue commissioned by Mrs Owen arrived in Scotland, on its way to Iona.

The details of how the transaction for the Iona statue were made are somewhat sketchy. It seems that Mrs Owen approached George MacLeod, offering to make a substantial donation to the work of the Community, provided he could find the money for the statue. At first reluctant to spend money on a statue, George consulted Sir Kenneth Clark as to the quality of the work and the standing of the sculptor. On being assured of its artistic worth, George then did what he regularly did – he approached one of the richest men he knew. That man was Sir John Mactaggart, and he too is an interesting part of the story.

John Mactaggart was born in 1867 in Glasgow. His parents had come from

Campbeltown in Kintyre and settled in the Anderston district of the city, where his father worked as a coppersmith. By 1901, Mactaggart had his own building company, and went on to become one of the most successful builders and developers in Scotland. In the 1920s, he built some 1500 houses in the Mosspark area of the city, and some 6,000 houses in King's Park, building them with gardens, because he believed that everyone should have their own green space. He bought Aikenhead House, a fine Georgian mansion in what was then the outskirts of the city, surrounded by the policies of King's Park. (The house still stands, divided into spacious flats. Mactaggart gifted the park to the City in 1930, and so it remains today, its walled garden one of the city's treasures.)

All his days, Sir John was a staunch socialist. He was the first Treasurer of the Scottish Labour Party under Keir Hardie. His granddaughter, Fiona Mactaggart, is presently Labour MP for Slough. King's Park Parish Church (of which I was Minister from 1979–2006) contains stained-glass windows given by the Mactaggart family. The chancel window commemorates Sir John's first wife, Margaret, who died in 1927. Two other windows commemorate Sir John, who died in 1956, and his second wife, Lady Lena Mactaggart, who died in November 1958. These dates are significant. The record shows that the statue was gifted by Sir John and Lady Mactaggart in 1956, which means that the gifting of the statue might well have been one of the last things Sir John did. And Lady Mactaggart died without ever seeing the statue in its place in Iona.

One final element in the story concerns its journey. Another of George MacLeod's friends – unnamed – who owned a shipping line, agreed to transport the statue in his ships without charge, provided time was not important. According to George's account, the statue left New York in December 1957.

For a whole year, 'Our Lady of Jubilation' sailed a good many of the seven seas, before her odyssey ended, at Christmas 1958.

In these stories of the people connected with the statue, it seems to me that we can see many of the central issues which, because of its theology of incarnation, the Iona Community continues to wrestle – peace and justice, violence and reconciliation; inter-church and interfaith relations; racist ideologies, asylum seekers, refugees; poverty, social policies, housing, homelessness; industry, trade, fairtrade, international debt, economic slavery; human community and the future of the planet – to name but a few. And in the statue itself, we have, I believe, a symbol which summons us to these issues with renewed commitment. For what does 'Our Lady of Jubilation' have to be jubilant about? It has to do ultimately with hope. In Leith Fisher's commentary on St Luke's Gospel, he says of the Magnificat: 'This heart-warming, soul-soaring song rightly belongs within the Church's communal praise-giving, expressing as it so powerfully does the hope of all God's people.' (*The Widening Road: from Bethlehem to Emmaus*, p.12). Call it what we will, the statue in the Cloisters, the symbolic place of the common life, continues to call us to the realisation of that hope, grounded as it is in the humanity of God.

Stewart Smith

*New Harmony: www-lib.iupui.edu/kade/newharmony/home.html*

*New Lanark: www.newlanark.org*

*The Iona Community: www.iona.org.uk*

# LIGHT OF THE WORLD

Numbers 24:17

Isaiah 9:2; 42:6–7; 49:6; 53:11

Malachi 4:2

John 1:4–9; 8:12; 9:5; 12:35–36, 46

Matthew 4:16; 17:2

Luke 1:78–79; 2:32

Acts 13:47

2 Corinthians 4:6

Hebrews 1:3

Revelations 1:16; 22:16

# BRIGHT AND AMAZING GOD

We believe in a bright and amazing God,
who has been to the depths of despair
on our behalf;
who has risen in splendour and majesty;
who decorates the universe
with sparkling water, clear white light,
twinkling stars and sharp colours,
over and over again.

We believe that Jesus is the light of the world;
that God believes in us, and trusts us,
even though we make the same mistakes
over and over again.

We commit ourselves
to Jesus
to one another as brothers and sisters,
and to the Maker's business in the world.
God said: Let there be light.
Amen

Affirmation written on Iona for a 'fireworks service'

# SOURCES AND ACKNOWLEDGEMENTS

Bible passages from the NRSV and the Good News Bible

'We believe in the Holy Spirit …' – by Dorothy McRae-McMahon, from *Liturgies for the Journey of Life*, Dorothy McRae-McMahon, SPCK, 2000

'An Ecumenical Accompanier in East Jerusalem' – © Elizabeth Burroughs. This poem was a winner of the 2008 Coracle Poetry Contest (on the theme of peace). Coracle is the magazine of the Iona Community www.iona.org.uk

'Awake out of sleep' – by George MacLeod, from *The Whole Earth Shall Cry Glory: Iona Prayers*, Wild Goose Publications, 1985 and 2007 © Iona Community

'I believe passionately in the power of non-violence …' – Extract from the 2004 Gandhi Foundation International Peace Award lecture. The 2004 Gandhi Foundation International Peace Award was given to Iona Community members Ellen Moxley and Helen Steven.

'The map of non-violence', extract from the talk 'A Religious Perspective on Peacemaking', by Kathy Galloway © Kathy Galloway

'He comes the broken hearts to heal … ' – by Graham Kendrick, from 'Make Way, Make Way' © 1986 Thankyou Music

'Sing out my soul, sing of the holiness of God' – by Janet Morley, from *All Desires Known*, 3rd edition, 2005, SPCK. Used by permission of Janet Morley.

SIPRI statistics used by permission of Stockholm International Peace

Research Institute www.sipri.org

'Bright and amazing God' – by Helen Lambie, *Iona Abbey Worship Book*, Wild Goose Publications, 2001 © Iona Community

# CONTRIBUTORS

Ruth Burgess is a writer and editor. She enjoys fireworks, growing things and walking in the woods and along the beach. She is a member of the Iona Community.

Elizabeth Burroughs is a retired GP, who now works part-time as a hospice doctor. She lives in St Austell, Cornwall where she is a Methodist Local Preacher and a Fair Trader and is involved in ecumenical projects in the town. She has served twice as an Ecumenical Accompanier in Israel-Palestine – in Bethlehem during the hot summer of 2006 and in Jerusalem during the mild winter of 2008–9.

David J.M. Coleman is an Iona Community member and URC minister, married to and job-sharing with Zam Walker, at Brighthelm Church in Brighton, father to Taliesin and Melangell. He is a digital artist, writer and occasional pod/broadcaster as well as pictures editor for the Christian magazine *Magnet*. He longs to see one united inclusive free catholic Church.

Ian M Fraser has been a pastor-labourer in heavy industry, a parish minister, Warden of Scottish Churches House, an Executive Secretary of the World Council of Churches, and Dean and Head of the Department of Mission at Selly Oak Colleges, Birmingham. He is the author of nineteen books, including *Strange Fire*, *The Way Ahead: Grown-up Christians*, *Living a Countersign: From Iona to Basic Christian Communities* and *Reinventing Theology*, which is used as a standard theological sourcebook around the world (www.ionabooks.com). Throughout his life Ian has travelled the globe, alone and with his wife, Margaret, visiting basic Christian communities.

Kathy Galloway is a former Leader of the Iona Community.

John Harvey is a retired minister living and working in Glasgow, mainly in anti-poverty activities. He is a member of the Iona Community.

George MacLeod is the Founder of the Iona Community. Born just before the start of the 20th century into a famous ecclesiastical dynasty, he became increasingly aware of 'two nations', the rich and the poor. Awarded the Military Cross for bravery in the First World War, he moved inexorably towards socialism and pacifism during the depression years, as his theology became more mystical, cosmic and political. Many lives were changed by MacLeod's spine-tingling sermons, and many more by his personal example.

Peter Millar is a former Warden of Iona Abbey and is a well-known writer and campaigner for global justice.

Neil Paynter has been a farm labourer, a fruit-picker, a teacher, a security guard (reluctantly), a nurse's aide, a night shelter worker, a mental health support worker, a bookseller, a hospital cleaner, a stand-up comedian, a musician and an editor. He lived for four years on Iona as part of the Iona Community's Resident Group. He lives in Biggar with his partner Helen, his mother and Stevie, his cat.

Jan Sutch Pickard – 'I am a writer and storyteller, living on Mull. A few years ago I spent six years working in the Iona Community's Centres, latterly as Warden of the Abbey. Since then I've served on the Ecumenical Accompaniment Programme in Palestine and Israel, continuing a commitment to life in community, which is also relevant to life among neighbours in a small village.'

David Rhodes, a former journalist and minister, is best known for his books on social justice and on the idea that the Gospel is good news from those we call the poor. While working for the social justice project Faith in Leeds he began running inner-city 'retreats on the streets' to help Christians focus on God's love for the marginalised.

Stewart Smith is a minister of the Church of Scotland. Ordained in 1966, he has served in three parishes: Greenock: St Ninian's, Renton Trinity and King's Park Parish Church, Glasgow. Now retired, he is acting as pastoral assistant in East Kilbride Old Parish. He is married to Mary, and they have a daughter and a son, and two granddaughters. Stewart has been a member of the Iona Community since 1964.

Neil Squires is a member of the Iona Community.

Helen Steven is a member of the Iona Community.

Lotte Webb is Assistant Chaplain at St Mary's University College and an Associate member of the Iona Community. Among other things she has worked in youth ministry, school chaplaincy, as Iona Abbey Programme Worker and as a volunteer teacher for the Deep Griha Society in the slums of India.

# THE IONA COMMUNITY IS:

- An ecumenical movement of men and women from different walks of life and different traditions in the Christian church
- Committed to the gospel of Jesus Christ, and to following where that leads, even into the unknown
- Engaged together, and with people of goodwill across the world, in acting, reflecting and praying for justice, peace and the integrity of creation
- Convinced that the inclusive community it seeks must be embodied in the community it practises

Together with its staff, the community is responsible for:

- The islands residential centres of Iona Abbey, the MacLeod Centre on Iona, and Camas Adventure Centre on the Ross of Mull

and in Glasgow:
- The administration of the Community
- Work with young people
- A publishing house, Wild Goose Publications
- Its association in the revitalising of worship with the Wild Goose Resource Group

The Iona Community was founded in Glasgow in 1938 by George MacLeod, minister, visionary and prophetic witness for peace, in the context of the poverty and despair of the Depression. Its original task of rebuilding the monastic ruins of Iona Abbey became a sign of hopeful rebuilding of community in Scotland and beyond. Today, it consists of about 280 Members, mostly in Britain, and 1500 Associate Members, with 1400 Friends worldwide. Together and apart, the community 'follows the light it has, and prays for more light'.

For information on the Iona Community contact:
The Iona Community, Fourth Floor, Savoy House,
140 Sauchiehall Street, Glasgow G2 3DH, UK.
Phone: 0141 332 6343
e-mail: admin@iona.org.uk; web: www.iona.org.uk

For enquiries about visiting Iona, please contact:
Iona Abbey, Isle of Iona, Argyll PA76 6SN, UK.
Phone: 01681 700404

For books, CDs & digital downloads published by Wild Goose Publications:
www.ionabooks.com

Wild Goose Publications, the publishing house of the Iona Community established in the Celtic Christian tradition of Saint Columba, produces books, CDs and digital downloads on:

- holistic spirituality
- social justice
- political and peace issues
- healing
- innovative approaches to worship
- song in worship, including the work of the Wild Goose Resource Group
- material for meditation and reflection

For more information, please contact us at:

Wild Goose Publications
Fourth Floor, Savoy House
140 Sauchiehall Street,
Glasgow G2 3DH, UK

Tel. +44 (0)141 332 6292
Fax +44 (0)141 332 1090
e-mail: admin@ionabooks.com

or visit our website at
www.ionabooks.com
for details of all our products and online sales